Hungry for
Worship

Also by Dr. Frank S. Page

The Nehemiah Factor: 16 Vital Keys to Living Like a Missional Leader

Hungry for
Worship

Challenges
and Solutions
for Today's Church

Frank S. Page and L. Lavon Gray

NEW HOPE
PUBLISHERS
Gospel-Centered. Missions-Driven.

BIRMINGHAM, ALABAMA

New Hope® Publishers
PO Box 12065
Birmingham, AL 35202-2065
NewHopeDigital.com
New Hope Publishers is a division of WMU®.

Library of Congress Control Number: 2013955343

Unless otherwise noted, Scripture quotations are taken from the Holman Christian
Standard Bible © copyright 2000 by Holman Bible Publishers. Used by permission.
    Scripture quotations marked NIV are taken from the HOLY BIBLE, NEW INTERNATIONAL
VERSION®. NIV®. Copyright© 1973, 1978, 1984, 2011 by Biblica, Inc.® Used by permission. All
rights reserved worldwide.
    Scripture quotations marked KJV are taken from The Holy Bible, King James Version.
    Scripture quotations marked NKJV are taken from the New King James Version.
Copyright © 1982 by Thomas Nelson, Inc. Used by permission. All rights reserved.

Cover design by: Michel Lê
Interior design by: Glynese Northam

ISBN-10: 1-59669-407-6
ISBN-13: 978-1-59669-407-1

N144113 • 0514 • 3M1

Dedication

This book is dedicated to worship pastors who lead in worship from the overflow of their personal walk with God—keep pursuing the call!

From Frank

I dedicate this work to the glory of our Lord, who is worthy of worship! In Psalm 42, He shows us that worship must be expectant, must be honest, must be thorough, and must be connected. Let us continue to grow in our worship of Him until the day when we are worshipping Him in His presence, fully and finally.

From Lavon

To my late mother, Nita, who set no limits on our success. To my three daughters who bring so much joy to my life—Kayla, Lizzie, and Katibeth. Remember who you are and whose you are! To Wendy, my constant encourager and best friend

Contents

9   FOREWORDS BY ED STETZER AND MIKE HARLAND

15   PREFACE

17   INTRODUCTION

23   CHAPTER 1: Worship as the "Golden Calf"
Churches Worshipping Worship

35   CHAPTER 2: Have It Your Way
Consumerism and Age-Segregated Worship

55   CHAPTER 3: The American Idol Experience
Performance-Driven Worship

71   CHAPTER 4: The Worship Mirage
Training Worship Leaders to Lead Churches That Don't Exist

89   CHAPTER 5: Worship Under a Flag of Truce
Navigating a Postworship War Culture

107   CHAPTER 6: Back from the Dead
The Reemergence of the Choir in Modern Worship

123   CHAPTER 7: A Theological Melting Pot
The Loss of Theological Distinctiveness

141   CHAPTER 8: Worship Leader, Version 2.0
              The Loss of the Minister of Music as a Lifelong Calling

157   CHAPTER 9: Multisensory Overload
              Worship in a Technology-Driven Culture

173   CHAPTER 10: Every Nation, Every Tribe
              The Emergence of Multicultural Worship

189   NOTES

Foreword

I've always loved worship.

As a failed worship leader (every church planter has to play guitar, right?), I found worship both meaningful and powerful. Some of those times are when I am by myself—worship dominates my personal prayertime. Then there is corporate worship, which can be a great opportunity, but also a great challenge at times.

For many of us, few things are as meaningful and formative as moments spent in corporate worship. Churches spend countless hours and dollars to create environments where voices can be raised in song and hearts lifted in prayer. My church does and, probably, so does yours.

The prominence of worship in our churches is no accident. We serve a God who is worthy of worship and praise. In the Old Testament, they prepared and planned for worship and we should do no less. Often, though, these times of praise and worship become forums driven by consumerism rather than gratitude, and opinion rather than orthodoxy.

Churches that embrace God-centered worship are doing three things: they are keeping the focus on Creator rather than the creatures, they are giving multiple generations present an opportunity to worship God, and they are pointing people (lost and believers) to Jesus as they equip the hearts as well as the minds of the saints.

To do that, I encourage you to consider three questions:

1. What does the Bible say to include in your worship?
Instead of asking, "What could we include?" start with what *must* be a part of corporate worship according to the Scriptures (singing, teaching, reading of Scripture, etc.) and go from there.

In seeking to determine what is the right music for a church, it is important that we apply biblical principles to evaluate our music. That is not always easy, as the Bible contains no music notes and God indicates no musical preferences. Music has always been a struggle within the church.

It seems odd to hear Christians today insist that a certain style of music is best or act as if the recent "worship wars" were an anomaly in church history. Any Christian who knows our past would know that neither of those is the case.

One way we can avoid some of these conflicts is to educate our churches on exactly what the Bible says about worship and move from that shared foundation.

2. How can I do biblically commanded worship in culturally appropriate ways?

Rather than asking, "What would be trendy?" consider what would be appropriate for the culture in which God has placed you. Don't do a thing just because you can or because you always have, but do what you do in culturally relevant ways—musical style, timing, format, etc.

As one who enjoys worship in its many forms, I appreciate pastors and worship leaders who find ways to incorporate creative elements into a worship service. I appreciate efforts that hold history in one hand and current culture in the other, lifting both hands up to the One who was and is and is to come.

When you are or your church is crafting worship and music, it is important that you think through the issues of contextualization and theology. There must be a balance in your music and your methodology. You may have the freedom to choose, but use discernment to choose wisely.

3. What will help people in this culture and time worship in Spirit and in Truth?

Don't ask, "What do I like?" because it is impossible to please everyone. Ultimately, someone in your church is going to sacrifice their preferences so ask what fits best in your community and (after answering questions one and two) go with that.

Music can be one of the most controversial issues in the body of Christ. Each person has his or her own unique taste. Christians listen to, enjoy, and are edified by all types of music. Yet when they demand their preferences over the preference of others, worship becomes about *me* rather than *He*.

In addition, many twenty-first-century churches are torn between the generations present in their congregation and the culture outside of their walls. They strive to appeal to both, and often in their zeal to be relevant they lose sight of the object of their worship. Others choose comfort over culture and are content to turn a blind eye to the call to contextualize. It's a tricky balance, but one worth finding.

THE PURPOSE OF OUR WORSHIP

Any musical style or worship model must take into account that the audience of Christian worship and the object of Christian worship should be the same. If we craft our worship for a human audience rather than a Divine audience, we often fall into worshipping the human rather than the Divine.

To avoid the pitfalls, connect with culture, remain biblical, and point to Christ, it takes work. It's worth the time and planning, however, to do worship right. With a humble spirit focused on others, and a worshipful spirit desiring to honor God, worship can (and will be) biblical, meaningful, and powerful.

In *Hungry for Worship: Challenges and Solutions for Today's Church,* Lavon Gray and Frank Page provide us a guidebook to navigate these issues. In the times we find ourselves, we need such guidebooks—we're hungry for worship, but need to think more deeply, biblically, and missiologically as we engage in it.

I love worship enough to know we need to think about it discerningly— and I am thankful Gray and Page show us how.

Ed Stetzer
President, LifeWay Research

Foreword

It's amazing how the passing of time allows for perspective to change the way we think about things. For instance, when my first child was born, the unwritten rule was that you should never leave a baby on his back—he could choke on something. But by the time my youngest son was born nine years later, the rule had totally changed. We were told to never leave that child on his stomach—he could suffocate. Amazing.

So, here we are in the second decade of the twenty-first century, and perspectives about worship are still evolving in the church. It seems after 25-plus years of a so-called worship movement the opinions and practices of worship are more fractured than ever—sometimes even inside a single group of Christians in a church.

The question rising up in pastor's offices and worship communities of our churches these days is this: after many years of the so-called worship movement and the many changes in church music it brought us, what difference has it made in our the lives of our people?

The questions continue: for all the worship we have generated, and with all of our emphasis on creating authentic communities of Christians worshipping in spirit and truth, how much more effective is the church in reaching the world with the gospel and living as disciples growing in faith? We fought the "worship wars" and paid for them in blood. What has been the outcome? I mean, we closed up the organ and picked up a guitar, so we are now having a true revival, right (tongue firmly planted in cheek)?

This important book goes right after the implications of these questions. And it does so with a unique and balanced perspective from both a widely respected senior pastor and a seasoned veteran of worship-and-music ministry. These two church leaders answer these questions with an even more important one: what does the Bible say about all of this?

Hungry for Worship is not just another worship book. It is an important answer to the questions about worship on the hearts and minds of the modern church. And it's not just a book with another set of opinions on the subject. It is a serious attempt to gain a biblical perspective on these issues from two students of the Word and servants of the church.

The churches we serve are precious, just as my children were when they were infants. If something is happening in the worship experiences of our churches that could do harm to His bride, we had better figure out what God's Word has to say in this essential area of church life. *Hungry for Worship* is here to help.

Mike Harland

Director, LifeWay Worship

Preface

Most churches are comprised of multiple generations, each group having specific characteristics and preferences. The worship challenges over the next decade will require church leaders to understand specific traits related to each generation. Throughout *Hungry for Worship*, we use the following designations, as outlined by Thom S. Rainer and Jess W. Rainer in *The Millennials: Connecting to America's Largest Generation*, when referring to these groups. While these are by no means exhaustive, these designations will help the reader understand age breakdowns and generational characteristics as we discuss various topics.

Builders: Though once an inclusive term, demographers often divide this group into two categories: the GI generation (1904–24) and the silent generation (1925–45). The GI generation was influenced by two events: the Great Depression and World War II, and produced some of the "most powerful people our nation has known." Few of this generation are still living, but their influence was significant. The majority of the silent generation, sometimes referred to as the swing generation, is now over 70 years old. Often characterized by affluence, some demographers suggest "this group may be the last to generation to enjoy affluence in their retirement years."

Boomers: The people born in the years following World War II (1946–64) are called the boomer generation. Born during a time of American prosperity, boomers are often well-educated, idealistic, and tolerant of many different lifestyles. "The majority of boomers were raised by stay-at-home mothers who were younger than mothers with children at home today. They are the Woodstock and Vietnam generation that believed their way was *the* way. . . . By 1995 three out of ten living Americans were boomers."

Busters: People born during the next two decades (1965–79) are called baby busters because of the decline in live births from the previous generation. Now commonly referred to Gen X, this generation grew up in a world different from that of any previous generation, with many coming from broken homes and entering the workforce in an unstable economic environment. Though sometimes accused of having a poor work ethic, this generation is "no less diligent than any previous generation, especially the boomers."

Millennials: People born between 1980 and 2000 received their designation because they were the first generation to come of age in the new millennium. Nearly 80 million strong, they are the largest generation in American history. Millennials were reared in the digital age, with computers as a way of life. They are experts at multitasking and communicate through cell phones, text messaging, and social media. This group will exert enormous influence on worship approaches over the next decade, if for no other reason than their sheer size. Thom Rainer points out that between 1980 and 2000, nearly 78 million live births took place. This is 2 million more live births than the boomer generation, making the millennials "too big to ignore." Rainer goes on to identify three key traits of the millennial generation:

- *Value education.* In 2007, the first year the 25- to 29-year-old group was entirely comprised of millennials, 30 percent had attained a college degree.
- *Tarry to marry.* Millennials marry much later in life, if at all, than in previous generations. Perhaps one reason why is because about 65 percent choose to cohabitate, at least once, prior to marriage.
- *Reflect diversity.* Millennials are the most diverse generation in American history, representing a shrinking Anglo population and a growing Hispanic, Black, and Asian demographic.

Introduction

A WORD FROM FRANK

A guy is driving around and he sees a sign in front of a house, "Talking Dog for Sale." He rings the bell, and the owner tells him the dog is in the backyard. The guy goes around the house and into the backyard and sees a handsome Labrador retriever sitting there.

"You talk?" he asks. "Yep," the Lab replies. "So, what's your story?"

The Lab looks up and says, "Well, I discovered that I could talk when I was pretty young, and I wanted to help the government. So I told the CIA about my gift, and in no time at all, they had me jetting from country to country, sitting in rooms with spies and world leaders, because no one figured a dog would be eavesdropping.

I was one of their most valuable spies for eight years running. But, the jetting around really tired me out, and I knew I wasn't getting any younger, so I wanted to settle down. I signed up for a job at the airport to do some undercover security work, mostly wandering near suspicious characters and listening in on their conversations. I uncovered some incredible dealings and was awarded a batch of medals. I got married, had a mess of puppies, and now, I'm just retired."

The guy is amazed. He goes back in and asks the owner what he wants for the dog. "Ten dollars," says the owner.

The guy says, "This dog is amazing! Why on earth are you selling him for so cheap?"

"Because he's a liar. He didn't do any of that stuff."

I love that story! However, it is much too indicative of where we are in regard to our claims and boasts about worship. We talk much about it and do very little of it. It has become a big claim in the twenty-first-century

17

church; but, based on the reality of people's lives, the worship that we claim to be experiencing is not truly affecting the quality of our lives, our families, and our witness.

Hungry for Worship is indeed a challenge to all of us. It is a challenge to our churches, to our entities and to our educational institutions. It is a challenge to every believer to look seriously at how he or she worships.

I want to say how privileged I have been to work with Dr. Lavon Gray on this project. It has stretched me. We do not always agree, but I have found, much to my dismay, that I have come to agree with him much more than I would ever like him to know. He is a dear friend and I love him and his family unconditionally.

I want to say a word of thanks to all the churches that I have ever pastored. I've learned much about worship through my experience with them. Most recently, I have been privileged to be a transitional pastor in two separate churches. Both have been challenging yet rewarding experiences. I spent more than two years helping the First Baptist Church of Jackson, Mississippi, where Lavon Gray also served as minister of music and worship. What a ride that was! I grew to love those people so dearly and saw God's hand at work in helping that church prepare for their new pastor. I also have served the First Baptist Church of North Augusta, South Carolina, a church once served by my mentor, Dr. Charles Page. They are a church filled with dear people who truly want to follow our Lord in worship and ministry. It has been my privilege and honor to serve them as well.

Prior to that, I pastored for more than 34 years in churches throughout the nation. To say that I have grown in my understanding of worship and worship leadership by serving them is an understatement. I am thankful for the privilege of serving, but also thankful for their patience in putting up with me in my always expanding learning curve.

I also would like to say a word of thanks to my wife, Dayle, and my sweet daughters, Melissa, Laura, and Allison. While Melissa no longer is with us on earth, I will never forget how much she loved to worship. She had a freedom that encouraged us all. Our family is now joined by grandsons whom we love and adore. We deeply want them to learn how to worship our Lord in power, in strength, and in freedom. We want them to see that worship is not just something we do, but it is something that we are.

A WORD FROM LAVON

During my high school days, my friends and I decided to "opt out" of school to spend the day "floatin' the river." Not surprisingly, ten or so high school boys sneaking off together for a self-designated skip day was more about testosterone than good sense. My canoe partner was "Jason" (not his real name but we will go with that in order to protect the guilty). Jason and I played basketball for our school. He was an outstanding player who demonstrated his athletic prowess game after game, and was the all-time leading scorer in our high school's storied history. Jason amazed me with his ability to stay calm in the tensest situations. He always managed to sink the shot we needed. With Jason in my canoe, I knew our fellow truants would be mesmerized by our nautical abilities!

Everything went great for the first half of the trip, but suddenly our canoe began to swerve out of control. (Did I mention neither of us had ever even been in a canoe?) As we neared the bank, the canoe brushed against an old tree, and into the boat dropped one of my worst nightmares: a snake. Honestly, Jason and I had never really discussed snakes—it simply had not been necessary! But now, my brave friend—the basketball hero who led us to victory in game after game, who stared the enemy in the eye and hit game-winning shots—did the most unimaginable thing. Jason stood up in the canoe (a big no-no), pulled out a single-action revolver (I certainly did not know he had that on him!), and rapidly unloaded the pistol in a flurry of gunshots and smoke with expertise placing him somewhere between John Wayne and Barney Fife!

By the time the gunfire ended, I was standing on the bank (did I say I was scared of snakes? I also could swim a lot faster than Jason!) and watched in amazement as our canoe filled with water and sank to the bottom of the river. Trust me—a boat with six bullet holes sinks amazingly quickly! Jason's ill-fated decision resulted in us carrying the gunshot-ridden canoe back to the pick-up point and explaining to the owner why the bottom of what was perfectly good rental property was blown out. Plus, we had to cough up the cash to pay him for the incapacitated vessel. That day I made this commitment: I would *always* stop my friends from shooting holes in the boat . . . especially if I was in it! That is why we write this book.

The next decade presents enormous challenges for churches in the area of worship. Decades of "worship wars" have left many congregations shell-shocked and uncertain of their core identities. Church music and worship education continues to lag years behind actual church practice, leaving many worship pastors with minimal theological training. These with other factors including church consumerism, performance-driven worship, and the changing demographic landscape of our communities raise important issues for church leaders that must be addressed.

Hungry for Worship is not a systematic how-to manual. Rather, it is a tool to prompt discussion and deeper thought on these important issues. The challenges presented are broad yet not exhaustive. *Hungry for Worship* identifies ten real challenges facing churches in their search for impact and relevance in the twenty-first century. Dr. Page and I spent many hours discussing these challenges, often revising our opinions in light of biblical truth and actual church practice. The topics, by design, are open-ended in order to promote ongoing dialogue among church leaders. We do not have all the answers, but we pray this book will facilitate important discussions moving forward.

I had the privilege of serving with Dr. Frank Page at two different churches: First Baptist Church in Taylors, South Carolina, and First Baptist Church in Jackson, Mississippi. He is a model pastor and denominational leader, but most importantly a dear friend. This work is much stronger because of his input, and it was a privilege to cowrite with him.

Dr. Vernon Whaley, dean of the School of Music at Liberty University, has a keen understanding of the challenges facing institutions of higher education in the area of worship education. Liberty University has allowed Vernon to lead the way in overhauling outdated educational approaches for the next generation of worship leaders. Much of the content in the chapter entitled, "The Worship Mirage," was directly influenced by Vernon and his leadership at Liberty. I am deeply thankful for his long friendship and that he allowed us to pick his brain on this important subject.

Over the years many pastors, teachers, and professors helped shape my views on worship and ministry. Some of these include: L. Graham Smith, Sullen Morrison, Dr. Benjamin Harlan, Dr. Stanley Moore, Dr. Bruce Leafblad, and the late Dr. Lyndel Vaught. I will forever be thankful for their influence on my life and ministry.

Andrea Mullins and the team at New Hope Publishers provided consistent encouragement throughout the writing process. Joyce Dinkins and the entire editorial team helped shape the content into a clear, comprehendible message. Thank you for your excellent work.

My dear friend Cille Litchfield played a central role in proofreading and serving as a sounding board to make sure our thoughts were being accurately communicated. Cille spent many hours suggesting revisions and ensuring the manuscript was tight.

I also want to thank Ed Stetzer and Mike Harland for writing the forewords. Their experience and insight were valuable as the final manuscript was developed.

Finally, my wife, Wendy, and daughters, Kayla, Lizzie, and Katibeth, make enormous sacrifices as my schedule takes me away from home much too often. For some reason they think I am awesome, something I am thankful for on a daily basis. There are no words to express my love and appreciation for their unwavering support.

As Christians we are called to be worshippers of the God of the universe. It is my prayer *Hungry for Worship* will encourage us in our pursuit of the Great Commandment.

Pursuing the call
LLG

CHAPTER 1

Worship as the "Golden Calf":

CHURCHES WORSHIPPING WORSHIP

Imagine for a moment you arrive at the church house this Sunday, Bible in hand and family in tow, ready for a great day of worship. As you enter the worship center things look like any other Sunday: preservice music is playing, people are greeting one another, the band is ready to go. At the appointed hour, however, things get weird. The worship leader steps into position carrying a statue, a golden calf just like the one you learned about as a child in Sunday School, and places it in the center of the platform. As the congregation audibly gasps, the worship leader invites the congregation to stand and worship this "thing," this inanimate object that carries no power or hope. Two things then happen: First, several deacons rush the platform, remove the idol, and chase the worship leader out the front door. Second, a medical team rushes to the pastor with a defibrillator unit to resuscitate him following cardiac arrest!

While this situation may seem outlandish, it is closer to reality than we might want to believe. In truth, we live in a land of idol worshippers. Over the past 30 years, a monumental shift of focus has placed a growing emphasis on the topic of worship, giving rise to countless books and articles, a plethora of conferences and training events, a new genre of worship consultants, as well as parachurch organizations and entire publishing houses singularly dedicated to the subject. Colleges and seminaries now offer degrees in worship studies/leadership. The subject of worship, almost without fail, surfaces in any church-related discussion.

While at first glance this is not bad, after all God instructed us to worship Him, it is theologically problematic when our approach to worship displaces the object of worship. Unfortunately, this is exactly where we find ourselves today. While we have not collected gold from our church members to use in forging literal idols, far too many of us have elevated our methodology of worship to golden calf status, sanctimoniously placing it on the altars of our churches. Our intentions may be honorable, but an idol is still an idol, and the end result is exactly the same!

When did we become idol worshippers? It happened when the method of worship became the priority of our churches. Many spend much more time promoting a style of worship than encouraging people to stand in the presence of God. And a lot of us have bought into the idea! This coming weekend countless people will leave our worship services and comment, "I loved the worship today," when they really mean they loved the music. Therein lies the problem: our churches are filled with people hungry for a specific worship style (traditional, contemporary, modern, alternative, coffeehouse, or whatever else) rather than a life-changing dialogue with God. In elevating musical styles, our churches have polarized the Bride of Christ and there is no one to blame but ourselves.

This polarization has resulted in the *worship wars* that have fractured congregations of all sizes and denominations for the past three decades. This term, although commonly used to describe these all too common church conflicts, has no basis in a biblical understanding of worship. The term strictly refers to differences in musical style. Today, churches fight musical style wars, not worship wars. Regardless of what we call them, these conflicts are only symptomatic of the real culprit: the displacement of God as the object of our worship.

The fact something is amiss is reflected in the questions we ask each other. Pastors, in the past, discussed with their peers how many baptisms their church had performed. Over the years that conversation morphed into asking how many people were in Sunday School or small groups. Today, the most common question from church leaders and church members alike, almost always is, How many did you have in worship?

While this change in dialogue may reflect simple shifts in emphasis, the change more likely emphasizes that numbers are all that really matter. When our primary focus is on numbers everything else becomes subservient, including how we worship, and, more importantly, how many people have been saved or been discipled. Worship is relegated to a church growth strategy rather than a time of communion with a Holy God.

WE ARE NOT THE FIRST

Our generation is not the first to struggle with idolatry. Throughout the Old Testament, the Israelites weaved back and forth between worship of Jehovah and worship of pagan gods. In each of these instances, the end result never was good. Christians must understand there are always significant consequences for displacing God as the object of worship.

To fully understand God's requirement that He be the only object of our worship, it helps to look at Moses and his worship encounters on Mount Sinai. In Exodus 19 we find Moses in the first of at least five Sinai worship experiences. In this initial experience, God initiates a dramatic dialogue with Moses:

> On the third day, when morning came, there was thunder and lightning, a thick cloud on the mountain, and a loud trumpet sound, so that all the people in the camp shuddered. Then Moses brought the people out of the camp to meet God, and they stood at the foot of the mountain. Mount Sinai was completely enveloped in smoke because the Lord came down on it in fire. Its smoke went up like a furnace, and the whole mountain shook violently. As the trumpet grew louder and louder, Moses spoke and God answered him in the thunder. The Lord came down on Mount Sinai, at the top of the mountain. Then the Lord summoned Moses to the top of the mountain, and he went up.
>
> (Exodus 19:16–20)

In the chapters that follow, God gave Moses the Ten Commandments, as well as additional laws to guide the lives and worship practices of the children of Israel. During these Sinai encounters, God described in detail the specifics for building the Tabernacle and its surrounding courtyard and outlined the entire sacrificial system. No detail was left to chance, with colors, types of cloth, and metals all intricately detailed by God. In these chapters, God defined and prescribed the worship practice of the Israelites leaving no margin of error. Finally, in Exodus 31:18, God gave Moses two stone tablets containing His laws, written by the His own finger. Moses was in the midst of the ultimate mountaintop experience. Too bad all was not well at the foot of the mountain!

The Israelites became impatient waiting on their leader. After all, 40 days and nights was a long time. While Moses worshipped in God's presence, life in the camp continued. With no direction, the people began to lose faith.

> When the people saw that Moses delayed in coming down from the mountain, they gathered around Aaron and said to him, "Come, make us a god who will go before us because this Moses, the man who brought us up from the land of Egypt—we don't know what has happened to him!" Then Aaron replied to them, "Take off the gold rings that are on the ears of your wives, your sons, and your daughters and bring them to me." So all the people took off the gold rings that were on their ears and brought them to Aaron. He took the gold from their hands, fashioned it with an engraving tool, and made it into an image of a calf. Then they said, "Israel, this is your God, who brought you up from the land of Egypt!"
>
> (32:1–4)

We do not know all the circumstances surrounding this shift in attitude, but Scripture clearly records the devastating outcome: God was not happy! Upon coming down from the mountain, Moses ground the idol into powder and forced the people to drink it. In the end, the Levites killed 3,000 Israelites, and God inflicted a plague on the entire nation because they sinned against Him. The Israelites faced very significant consequences for focusing on an incorrect object of worship. The same is true for us today.

A BIBLICAL RESPONSE

In Exodus 20:3 (NKJV) when God said, "You shall have no other gods before me," He meant it! This literally means nothing should take importance over the One True God. God so desires to have communion with us that He never allows anything to be placed above Him. When outlining the requirements of the Covenant to Moses, God made this strikingly clear: "You are never to bow down to another god because Yahweh, being jealous by nature, is a jealous God" (34:14). This idea that God is "jealous" can be difficult to understand, but C. H. Spurgeon gave clarity to this attribute when he stated in his sermon, "A Jealous God" (spurgeon.org/sermons):

> [The attribute of] jealousy is selected as some faint picture of that tender regard which God has for His own Deity, honor, and supremacy, and the holy indignation which he feels towards those who violate his laws, offend his majesty, or impeach his character. Not that God is jealous so as to bring him down to the likeness of men, but that this is the nearest idea we can form of what the Divine Being feels—if it be right to use even that word toward him— when he beholds his throne occupied by false gods, his dignity insulted, and his glory usurped by others.

Jesus, in the New Testament, underscored God's requirement that He not be displaced from His throne. In Matthew 22:34 we find the Pharisees approaching Jesus and asking, "Teacher, which is the greatest commandment?" His response is consistent with the theme of the Old Testament when He replies, "Love the Lord your God with all your heart, with all your soul, and with all your mind. This is the greatest and *most important* command" (22:37–38; author's emphasis). The word "greatest," translated from the original Greek superlative *megalh,* literally means "first in importance." In Jesus' response to the Pharisees, He affirms worship as our first priority.

In reality, however, many Christians get the cart ahead of the horse. Scripture clearly teaches there is an order of priorities for the church, and Jesus placed loving God at the top of that list. Worship serves as our lifeline to God. Without it we have no power to accomplish these tasks. In order for us to love people as ourselves, which Jesus established as the second and greatest commandment, we must see them through the eyes and heart of our Lord by having a heart like His. That only happens when we connect to Him through worship. Churches struggling with low or nonexistent conversions, lack of passion for missions and evangelism, and weak commitment to ministry should look first at their passion for worship. The reason there is no power: we are not connected to the Power Source.

Prioritizing loving God does not devalue the importance of missions and discipleship laid out in the Great Commission. However, in our effort to be "good Christians," many of us try to carry out these functions of the church but end up failing miserably. For example, as church leaders we have tried using guilt, the latest witness training methods, gimmicky outreach approaches such as Bring a Friend Day, and every other imaginable approach to force people to share their faith. How many churches using these tactics are actually reaching their communities for Christ? While all these tools have a place in training and inspiring us to share our faith, they tend to address the symptoms rather than the root problem.

Note the priority is worship . . . not music. God is to be the object of all our human emotions, energy and intellect, and will not tolerate being displaced from His throne by anyone—or anything—including our approach to worship no matter how well-intentioned.

𝄢 WHAT NOW?

INTENTIONAL DISCIPLESHIP

In reality most church members have little understanding of the biblical meaning and purpose of worship. Research by the Barna Group indicated only 29 percent of churchgoing adults understood worship was something that focused primarily on God. According to their report, almost half of congregants surveyed (47 percent) most likely understood worship as an activity undertaken for their personal benefit. One of every five attendees admitted they had no idea of the main purpose of worship.

As church leaders, we must develop an intentional strategy to disciple our ministry teams and congregations on the biblical role of worship. Obviously, a sermon series on the topic of worship can be effective if it is creative and focused. Other targeted discipleship opportunities can be effective when working with smaller groups. For example, you might start with a required training time for vocalists, instrumentalists, and worship team members. Use this time to train team members regarding expectations (i.e., attendance, rehearsal, spiritual disciplines) as well as clearly define their role as worship leaders (not performers). Other training opportunities could include weekly blogs or online devotionals, worship ministry retreats, or small-group Bible studies. Regardless of your approach, the key is to be intentional. Though it requires time and effort, your church will reap enormous benefits if your worship ministry has a common understanding of what God has called them to do in leading His people in worship.

MAKE PREACHING OF THE WORD OF GOD CENTRAL TO WORSHIP

Far too long many pastors have tried to shift the responsibility of growing the church away from the pulpit and onto the music. While music plays a critical role, its exaggerated importance by our modern church culture erroneously has elevated it to golden calf status. While probably true that many good sermons have been ruined by bad music, and many bad sermons made better by good music, it is the strength of the pulpit that determines the impact of your church. As the Apostle Paul reminded us, God uses the foolishness of preaching to save a lost world.

For since, in God's wisdom, the world did not know God through wisdom, God was pleased to save those who believe through the foolishness of the message preached. For the Jews ask for signs and the Greeks seek wisdom, but we preach Christ crucified, a stumbling block to the Jews and foolishness to the Gentiles. Yet to those who are called, both Jews and Greeks, Christ is God's power and God's wisdom, because God's foolishness is wiser than human wisdom, and God's weakness is stronger than human strength.

(1 Corinthians 1:21–25)

Many pastors unfortunately have forgotten this truth. Once, during a dinner conversation with Jim Whitmire, who served more than 30 years alongside Dr. Adrian Rogers at Bellevue Baptist Church in Cordova, Tennessee, the question was asked, "Jim, you worked with Dr. Rogers for over two decades. How many bad sermons did you hear him preach?" Whitmire looked up from his meal and without hesitation responded, "Not one. I never heard him preach a bad sermon!" Whitmire explained that in a church culture where many pastors blame their congregation's decline or lack of growth on the music, Rogers would never have taken that approach. To do that would have been an affront to God by devaluing the central role of the preached word.

While most pastors will never have the oratorical skills of Adrian Rogers, strong, authoritative, biblical preaching must once again become the priority in our churches. Music is important to our corporate worship, yet most people will make their decision on where to attend based on the strength of the pulpit. Research published by Thom S. Rainer indicates that 90 percent of unchurched people indicated the pastor or preaching is the number one factor impacting their choice of churches. Conversely, only 11 percent indicated that music was most important.

STOP MARKETING STYLE

If you do not believe churches are marketing style, take a few minutes and explore church websites or observe a few church signs. In a few minutes you see just how off track we really are. These are a few marketing lines from established churches across the country that illustrate how our approach to worship has replaced God as the object of our affection and attention:

- At 11:00 a.m. each Sunday, you can come experience contemporary worship.
- Our contemporary worship service provides an opportunity to experience energetic, band-oriented, spiritually fulfilling praise and worship in a modern environment.
- Sunday at 9:00 a.m. is our traditional worship service. This service is characterized by the hymns we've come to appreciate as a part of our heritage and faith, as well as by classic choruses, and will be accompanied by our dynamic celebration choir and orchestra.
- Experience our contemporary service. This service is led by a progressive worship band, and uses material from a variety of worship sources, including songs written by our own team of worship leaders.
- Each Sunday morning service incorporates different musical styles: 8:30 a.m. traditional with hymns and songs of the faith led by choir and orchestra, organ, and piano; 9:45 a.m. contemporary with energizing and uplifting music led by band, choir, and vocalists; and 11:15 a.m. modern with passionate, upbeat, band-led, creative media-rich experience.

In each of these examples, the focus is experiencing the approach to worship (i.e., the music). Nothing is said about experiencing God. We are marketing the wrong thing! While our motives may be pure, we have placed the focus on our methods, which most commonly means worship style. Is it any wonder that, according to LifeWay Research, 70 percent of young adults aged 23 to 30 stop attending church regularly for at least a year between ages 18–22? We asked them to buy into our methods rather than our Savior!

While there's nothing inherently wrong with describing different styles of services, it must be carefully done. We truly need to focus on why we come and what we do in proclaiming our Savior, not just how! Young adults look for authenticity more than any other single major generational group. They sense a lack of authenticity when we market a method instead of focusing on our Lord!

UNDERSTAND THE ROLE OF MUSIC IN WORSHIP

Contrary to popular opinion, music is not synonymous with worship. In our modern worship culture, due to marketing and branding, many have lost sight that music in worship is a functional art and never an end in itself. Never should there be music simply for the sake of the music.

Several years ago the Boston Pops Orchestra made a concert stop in Greenville, South Carolina, as part of their annual tour. That night's program included an assortment of movie themes from blockbusters such as *Star Wars*, *Raiders of the Lost Ark*, and *Superman*. As you can imagine, the evening was incredibly filled with music performed with a high degree of excellence. Even so, the music had no real purpose or function other than entertainment. It was music for the sake of music. In contrast, music in worship always has a higher function, yet it is not the goal.

As Christian musicians we can get so involved in perfecting the tool that we lose sight of what the tool was designed to do in the first place. Christian musicians must ask themselves some hard questions and may find they do not like the answers:

- Am I more passionate about music than I am about the God of the Ages?
- Do I spend as much time in prayer and Bible study as I do on rehearsing and leading?
- Is my role in the worship service a performance opportunity or a chance to lead people to the throne of God?
- If the music was gone, how strong would my faith commitment be?

Matt Redman's song, "The Heart of Worship," was birthed from a time when his home church, Soul Survivor, in Watford, England, asked these types of questions. It was during this time that Matt's pastor, Mike Pilavachi, discerned the church had lost their focus on God as the object of worship, so he made a brave call: he temporarily removed the sound system and band from the services. As Redman points out, "His point was that we'd lost our way in worship, and the way to get back to the heart would be to strip everything away." Over the following weeks, the people were asked to consider what they were bringing as an offering to God. This led to a time of spiritual renewal and a fresh encounter with God that changed the church in amazing ways. When the band and musicians were reintroduced some weeks later, the church had a new understanding role of music and worship. This journey prompted Redman to pen these words: "When the music fades, all is stripped away and I simply come . . . I'm coming back to the heart of worship, And it's all about You, Jesus." How would we react if the music were taken away? The answer to that question should help us understand whether music is a golden calf in our lives.

CONCLUSION

Several years ago the authors led a team on a missions project to Chang Mai, Thailand. There they visited a Buddhist temple on the outskirts of the city. As the team walked through the ornate structure, overlaid with gold and fine jewels and sitting high on a mountain, all around were people burning incense and bowing down before statues of Buddha. These people were sincere, energetic, and passionate . . . but the object of their worship had no power. It was an idol.

As Christians we must be hungry for worship! This means the passion of our lives must be the development of a love relationship with the living God through Jesus Christ. This is done first and foremost through our daily walk with Him in prayer, the study of His Word, and personal worship. Second, our corporate worship must become an overflow of our personal worship experiences where the primary focus is meeting with God. Third, our approach to worship must simply be a tool that allows us to experience the presence of God and grow in our relationship with Him. While our approach is important, it cannot be the primary focus of worship. That place is reserved for God Himself!

CHAPTER 2

Have It Your Way

CONSUMERISM AND AGE-SEGREGATED WORSHIP

The Worshipping Family: A Modern-Day Parable

On this Sunday morning, the Johnson family arrives at New Horizons Church (formerly Westside Baptist Church) with ten minutes to spare—a small miracle. Saturday and in fact their entire week was hectic. The day began with an early morning soccer game in which their youngest son, Brent, played goalie. Next came a noon piano recital for Jessica (the middle child). Then the family loaded the SUV and drove two hours for a football game at the state university where their oldest son, Andrew, is a senior. After the game, a losing effort, they drove back home, arriving sometime after midnight. Joe (the dad) was out of town working all week and Kelly (the mom) had PTA responsibilities on two nights. Describing the week as "hectic" was a monumental understatement. Although the Johnsons performed no chest bumps in the parking lot, making it to church at all, much less early, was a huge victory!

As the Johnsons enter the church facilities, silently wishing for ten more minutes of sleep, they hurriedly pass the high school worship area leaving Jessica, who plays keys for the student band, so she can rehearse for the contemporary service. A young man dressed in jeans, T-shirt, and flip-flops speaks to Joe as they pass in the hallway. He has no idea the young man is the new student pastor (actually not that new . . . he has been there six months), but Joe awkwardly acknowledges the greeting while lamenting the lax dress code of the student ministry.

The Johnsons (minus one) quickly move to the atrium outside the main sanctuary where Andrew heads off to attend the "modern" service in the fellowship hall. This service attended primarily by college students, features lights, smoke, and a rock band. This is the first time Andrew has been in church in months. Although active in the student ministry growing up, once college began, Sundays became his only day to sleep in. Besides, there are no churches in his college town that use music he likes. His parents don't know he's dropped out. This morning he will connect with old high school friends before heading back to campus after lunch.

The Johnsons (now minus two) enter the worship center for the traditional service and move to their customary pew. Brent, their seventh-grader, spots several of his middle school friends and joins them as they head for the balcony. Even though he doesn't like the "old music," he can hide in the back of the church and check out the latest app on his smartphone. After all, he can endure anything for an hour.

As the organ prelude ends, the Johnsons (now minus three) speak to a few folks seated near them while observing a slide on the big screen at the front of the sanctuary. The slide reads: "Welcome to New Horizons Church: A Place for Families." As the worship leader stands to lead the opening hymn, a sinking feeling that something just isn't right hits Joe.

♫ = ♩♪

While the Johnson family is fictional, the challenges highlighted are real. We stand on the threshold of one of the most significant crises in the history of the modern church: the unintended yet potentially devastating consequences of two decades of age-segregated worship. While the slogan Have It Your Way may work for Burger King, this approach to worship has been a disaster for the church. In an attempt to give people what they want, often at the exclusion of what they need, many churches bought into, or at least were influenced by, a consumer-driven approach. This focus on consumer preference fundamentally changed the way many churches operate, often leaving the body of Christ segregated by age and musical style preference. While this may not be true in smaller churches, it is a growing number and practice.

While consumerism impacts many areas of church life, it has significantly affected how most churches perceive and understand worship. All too often, the intended time of communion with God becomes relegated to a methodology for church growth. The effort to reach large numbers results in many churches offering worship buffets with multiple worship times defined by musical style. Some churches make this decision based on a sincere desire to reach their surrounding communities for Christ. For others, it is an attempt to meet the musical style preferences of all their members. Sometimes, it is a combination of the two. Each case, however, elevates personal preference to an unhealthy status.

Unfortunately, when left to our own preferences we often revert to what C. S. Lewis called chronological snobbery, where older generations only find value in the traditions and heritage of our faith, while younger generations only find relevance in what is current.[1] In the end, this division by churches into separate worship times, defined by musical styles, effectively began dismembering the body of Christ limb by limb.

Over the past 20 years, our churches have managed to raise a generation of young Christians with little connection to the body of Christ as a whole. Just as devastating, we patronized older generations with an environment of irrelevancy and self-centeredness by disconnecting them from modern movements of God. In many churches students attend worship on Sunday and Wednesday and never enter the main worship center or encounter a single senior adult. Likewise, senior adults, while active in church, never have interaction with students and young adults. This approach may successfully give people an exclusive diet of what they want, but it breeds dissension and is contradictory to Scripture. Students need the maturity and teaching of older generations to ground them in our historical and theological foundations. Likewise, more mature adults need exposure to the passion and energy of younger Christians. The church needs both perspectives to remain healthy.

This loss of connectivity between generations comes at a huge price: our inability to retain young Christians. LifeWay Research reported on lifeway.com that 70 percent of young adult Protestants aged 23 to 30 who attended church regularly in high school quit attending for one year between ages 18 and 22. Additionally, many young adults who identify themselves as Christians are either marginal Christians or Christians in name only. Some are simply indifferent to the church. The situation is lose-lose: we are not reaching the world for Christ, and we are losing our own children. Pastor, researcher, and president of LifeWay Research Ed Stetzer highlighted this failure when he stated:

> There is no easy way to say it, but it must be said. Parents and churches are not passing along a robust Christian faith and an accompanying commitment to the church. . . . Christian parents and churches need to ask the hard question, "What is it about our faith commitment that does not find root in the lives of our children?"

It is not just young Christians. Boomer and buster generations focus on their individual preferences through church shopping, thus encouraging churches to offer consumer-driven programming in order to keep members on their rolls. Dr. Albert Mohler Jr., president of the Southern Baptist Theological Seminary, lamented this fact when he stated:

> Far too many church members have become church shoppers. The biblical concept of ecclesiology has given way to a form of consumerism in which individuals shop around for the church that seems most to their liking at that moment. The issue can concern worship and music, relationships, teaching, or any number of other things. The pattern is the

same, however—people feel free to leave one congregation for another for virtually any reason, or no reason at all.

These trends, and no doubt other forces, directly resulted in a free fall in church membership and baptisms. According to North American Mission Board statistics, 70 percent of all Southern Baptist churches are declining or plateaued, while worship attendance and overall membership in the Southern Baptist Convention continue to decline.[2] In fact, in 2012 Southern Baptist baptisms dropped below 315,000 for the first time since 1948, confirming a two-decade downward trend. This stark decline in church membership most certainly contributed to 880 Southern Baptist churches closing their doors between the years 1999–2009. More sobering is the warning by Southern Baptist leaders that if these trends are left unchecked, half of all Southern Baptist churches will close their doors permanently by the year 2030. In an article called, "Curing Christians' Stats Abuse," Ed Stetzer observed:

> Mainline denominations are no longer bleeding; they are hemorrhaging. Increasingly, they are simply managing their decline. For evangelicals, the picture is better, but only in comparison to the mainline churches. Southern Baptists, composing the largest Protestant denomination in the U.S., have apparently peaked and are trending toward decline.

To fully grasp the magnitude of the crisis, we must remember these trends developed as the church made unprecedented efforts to be culturally relevant to busters and millennials. After spending millions of dollars and making monumental shifts in methodologies in pursuit of cultural relevance, the haunting question remains: why hasn't it worked?

While there are many contributing factors, one of the main culprits is our separation of the body of Christ through age-segregated worship. In the book *Sticky Faith,* authors Kara Powell, Brad Griffin, and Cheryl Crawford determined that involvement in worship that is multigenerational during the high school years is more consistently linked with mature faith in both high school and college than any other form of church participation.

> While small groups, mentoring, justice works, and a host of other youth ministry activities are important, the reality is that the challenges of kids, ministry programs, and spiritual development are far too complicated to be met with a single solution. The closest our research has come to that definitive silver bullet is this sticky finding: high school and college students who experience more intergenerational worship tend to have higher faith maturity. We found this to be true in our studies of both high school seniors and college freshmen.

DUMBING DOWN A GENERATION

While there have always been inherent dangers in style-driven and age-segregated worship approaches, the problem exponentially expands when the central message of the gospel is abandoned in order to be more relevant and user friendly. For years many church leaders raised the concern that we would raise a generation of believers with no theological foundations or understanding of key doctrinal beliefs. Unfortunately, we are now seeing more and more quantifiable evidence suggesting these concerns were merited.

For example, beginning in 2009, Louisiana College, a private Baptist college founded in 1906 and located in heart of the Bible Belt, administered to incoming freshmen a BASE (Belief Assessment of Spiritual Essentials) exam to determine how well they understand the essential doctrines of our Christian faith. These were not "lofty doctrines" but rather "essential gospel truths" that a person must understand and believe to consider themselves Christian. These included such things as humanity's sinful and lost condition, Jesus' identity as God, the necessity of faith in Jesus for salvation, and the Lord's bodily resurrection. The exam results are telling:

- Seventy-eight percent believed that all people are basically good and have no real need for a Savior.
- Sixty-five percent could not identify a simple definition of new birth in a multiple-choice question. They thought that being born again meant experiencing reincarnation or transmigration in which a person who died returns to earth in another life form so that they can make up for the sins of the past.
- Fifty-four percent thought faith in Jesus was unnecessary for salvation. In their view, as long as a person believes in a god and has fallen in love with him, her, or it, he is right with that god.
- Forty-two percent believed that people go to heaven because of their personal morality rather than Jesus' sacrificial death.
- Thirty-two percent did not know that Christianity affirms the deity of Jesus Christ, even though the New Testament repeatedly insists that faith in Jesus as God is necessary for salvation.
- Twenty-five percent did not know Christianity claims that Jesus literally rose from the dead.[3]

Overall, incoming freshmen at Louisiana College scored a dismal 67 percent on the BASE exam/questionnaire, despite that 90 percent of the incoming freshmen claim to be Christians and nearly 60 percent were reared in Southern Baptist churches.[4]

These results are not unique to Louisiana College. Churches all across the United States failed to teach and disciple an entire generation in the basic foundations of our faith. We have given them worship approaches that cater to their preferences and feel-good devotionals to get them in the door, and then failed to disciple them into spiritually mature followers of Christ. In a *USA Today* article entitled "Survey: 72% of Millennials 'More Spiritual than Religious,'" Thom Rainer, president of LifeWay Christian Resources, summed up the results of this "reach numbers at all cost" attitude when he said, "We have dumbed down what it means to be part of the church so much that it means almost nothing, even to people who already say they are part of the church. . . . If the trends continue, the Millennial generation will see churches closing as quickly as GM dealerships."

Our failed attempts to reach the millennials are illustrative of what Thomas Bergler, who teaches student ministry at Huntington University and serves as the associate senior editor of the *Journal of Youth Ministry*, calls the "juvenilization of American Christianity." According to Bergler:

> Juvenilization is the process by which the religious beliefs, practices, and developmental characteristics of adolescents become accepted as appropriate for adults. It began with the praiseworthy goal of adapting the faith to appeal to the young, which in fact revitalized American Christianity. But it has sometimes ended with both youth and adults embracing immature versions of the faith.

In a tongue-in-cheek description of a worship service that sounds all too familiar, he identifies characteristics of the student culture that have permeated modern worship practices, as well as the resulting spiritual immaturity:

> The house lights go down. Spinning, multicolored lights sweep the auditorium. A rock band launches into a rousing opening song. "Ignore everyone else, this time is just about you and Jesus," proclaims the lead singer. The music changes to a slow dance tune and the people sing about falling in love with Jesus. A guitarist sporting skinny jeans and a soul patch closes the worship set with a prayer beginning, "Hey God . . . " The spotlight then falls on the speaker, who tells entertaining stories, cracks a few jokes, and assures everyone that "God is not mad at you. He loves you unconditionally."
>
> Fifty or sixty years ago, these now commonplace elements of American church life were regularly found in youth groups but rarely in worship services and adult

activities. What happened? Beginning in the 1930s and 1940s, Christian teenagers and youth leaders staged a quiet revolution in American church life that led to what can properly be called the juvenilization of American Christianity. Today many Americans of all ages not only accept a Christianized version of adolescent narcissism, they often celebrate it as authentic spirituality. God, faith, and the church exist to help me with my problems. Religious institutions are bad; only my personal relationship with Jesus matters. If we believe that a mature faith involves more than good feelings, vague beliefs, and living whatever we want, we must conclude that juvenilization has revitalized American Christianity at the cost of leaving many individuals mired in spiritual immaturity.

A point of clarification: there is nothing scripturally wrong with intelligent lighting, electric guitars, or spiked hair. In fact, Scripture teaches the church to be relevant to the culture in which we live. In 1 Corinthians 9:22 (NIV), Paul explained this saying, "To the weak I became weak, to win the weak. I have become all things to all people so that by all possible means I might save some." With this understanding, however, comes a major caveat: we must never undermine the central message of the gospel. As Christian leaders we must make an unwavering commitment to disciple our people into mature followers of Christ. This presents a challenge in that it is difficult, if not impossible, to disciple immature Christians in environments that are age-homogenous. To effectively grow in our walk with Christ, we need to see our faith modeled and passed down. This happens best when done from one generation to another.

A BIBLICAL RESPONSE
GENERATION TO GENERATION

Students' and young adults' need for a multigenerational worship approach should come as no surprise. In Deuteronomy 6:4–9, Moses instructed the Israelites on the importance of teaching the precepts of their faith to younger generations:

> *These commandments that I give you today are to be on your hearts. Impress them on your children. Talk about them when you sit at home and when you walk along the road, when you lie down and when you get up. Tie them as symbols on your hands and bind them on your foreheads. Write them on the doorframes of your houses and on your gates.*

The passage, known as the Shema, serves as the centerpiece of the morning and evening prayers for Judaism and lays the foundation of their belief in Jehovah God (Yahweh). Most importantly, the Israelites were commanded to "Impress them on your children."

The importance of passing our faith from "generation to generation" can be found throughout Scripture. These are a few of the passages that underscore the importance of generational discipleship:

Psalm 145:4 (NIV)—"One generation commends your works to another; they tell of your mighty acts."

Deuteronomy 11:19 (NIV)—"Teach them to your children, talking about them when you sit at home and when you walk along the road, when you lie down and when you get up."

Psalm 78:4–5 (NIV)—"We will not hide them from their descendants; we will tell the next generation the praiseworthy deeds of the Lord, his power, and the wonders he has done. He decreed statutes for Jacob and established the law in Israel, which he commanded our fathers to teach their children."

Ephesians 6:4 (NIV)—"Fathers, do not exasperate your children; instead, bring them up in the training and instruction of the Lord."

Deuteronomy 4:9–10 (NIV)—"Only be careful, and watch yourselves closely so that you do not forget the things your eyes have seen or let them fade from your heart as long as you live. Teach them to your children and to their children after them. Remember the day you stood before the Lord your God at Horeb, when he said to me, 'Assemble the people before me to hear my words so that they may learn to revere me as long as they live in the land and may teach them to their children.'"

Deuteronomy 6:7 (NIV)—"Impress them on your children. Talk about them when you sit at home and when you walk along the road, when you lie down and when you get up."

Psalm 78:6 (NIV)—"So the next generation would know them, even the children yet to be born, and they in turn would tell their children."

Proverbs 22:6 (NIV)—"Start children off on the way they should go, and even when they are old they will not turn from it."

Isaiah 38:19 (NIV)—"The living, the living—they praise you, as I am doing today; parents tell their children about your faithfulness."

WHAT NOW?

With so much emphasis on musical style and worship approaches, how do we get our focus back on God as the object of worship? How can churches that have relegated worship to a church growth strategy redefine their identities? With our churches filled with people conditioned to their preferences, is unity even possible? It is one thing to talk about the importance of multi-generational worship. It is something totally different to successfully implement it. Though difficult, more and more churches are making the decision that the end result is worth the effort. While hard, it is not an impossible task.

LEAD IN FRONT OF THE BEAT

Musicians often will play or sing on the backside of the beat. The result is a dragging, muddy, lethargic, and unenergetic sound. This same risk exists in planning multigenerational worship. We should be leading our people to new and fresh encounters with a living God, on the front edge of what God is doing in our lives and churches. We need to lead in front of the beat.

This means we do not revert to an old musical arrangement simply because it requires little rehearsal, or use the same set list due to our lack of creativity and planning. To engage multiple ages in a unified worship experience, we must be continually learning and exploring new approaches to how we lead worship. As worshippers we must pray that God would give us a desire to experience the new and open our eyes to truths we have never seen. Leading in front of the beat can be scary because we often feel exposed. The flipside is we are forced to rely on God for direction as we seek creative and new ways to tell the timeless story of grace. The end result can be life-changing for everyone involved.

FOCUS ON THE HIGHEST COMMON DENOMINATOR—HYMNS

Creatively presented hymns can be one of the most important unifying elements in multigenerational worship. There are several reasons for this. First, older generations view hymns as "old friends" they've known their entire lives. Second, students and young adults who grew up in church are familiar with the texts and accept them as part of their Christian heritage. Third, those who are unchurched have no preference either way; they do not know if the songs are old or new. The key lies in the manner of presentation. Creative use of instruments and fresh arrangements can bring them to life and reintroduce them to our congregations. Also, the addition of a new chorus reframes an old hymn in a powerful way and can rearticulate a message that has been lost due to repeated use.

For many years worship leaders moved away from using hymns as part of modern worship approaches. That is no longer the case. In fact, in recent years, many Christian artists, including Chris Tomlin, Mandisa, Newsboys, Kari Jobe, Third Day, and David Crowder, released modern versions of hymns. In each case these fresh presentations of familiar material allow the lyrics to take on new meaning for the worshipper.

One of the highlights of teaching at Liberty University, the largest Christian university in the world, is the privilege of participating in convocation. Three times each week more than 12,000 students join together in a high-energy, passionate time of worship. While the singing is always powerful, it moves to a different level when the worship times include hymns such as "Amazing Grace" and "Jesus Paid It All." Creatively presented hymns are the unifying element—don't underestimate their importance!

UNDERSTAND YOUR CHURCH'S IDENTITY

Who are you as a church? Many churches are guilty of using a cookie-cutter approach when it comes to church identity. After all, if it works for someone else it should work for us, right? While appearing to be the easiest road to take, it sells churches short of the calling God placed on their ministries. God has a unique plan for every church and it is our job as leaders to clearly identify it. To accomplish that plan, you must first determine who you are.

For example, a new church start in California will have a different worship identity than a 175-year-old congregation in Mississippi. A worship ministry in rural Tennessee will have a different feel than one in urban Chicago. Diversity is a good thing and reflects the cultures in which we serve. The problems arise when worship leaders in Mississippi trade in their suits for shorts, or the church in Tennessee introduces a rap song they heard while in Chicago. It simply does not work.

There are several questions that can help us better understand how worship fits into the church's identity. Going through this process, while not complicated, can be gut-wrenching if we answer the questions honestly.

- What makes our worship ministry unique?
- Are we simply copying another church's approach?
- What resources (people, musical, artistic, financial, etc.) are available that will allow us to connect with our community?
- Are we being good stewards of those resources in leading people to the throne of God?

- Have we prayed for God's specific plan for our worship ministry?
- Are we planning worship experiences that are authentic and fresh?

Note that many churches have experienced problems, and some have even split, as a result of multiple worship identities operating within the same body. A convoluted identity presents obstacles to unifying the church family. Nail down who you are early in the process, and then work within that identify.

INTENTIONALLY RAISE UP SONGWRITERS
Many churches have found that their ability to form a unique worship identity is greatly enhanced by utilizing original songs written by members of their churches. While every song cannot be original, using materials that have been birthed as a result of what God is doing in your specific ministry can unify congregations around a common experience. Pastors and worship leaders are now focusing heavily on writing original songs, and that trend will continue to grow over the next decade. In fact, many churches now employ songwriters and arrangers to facilitate this movement, a major shift in the development of worship literature.

Prior to 1970, the vast majority of churches utilized common worship literature handed down from previous generations or written and composed by professional "hymnists" or musicians. Those days are gone. While many of our modern worship songs became popular because of artist recordings, oftentimes they were written by people outside the professional music culture. This is especially true of millennials, who often can be found with a guitar and notebook in hand, putting into song their latest experience on their Christian journey. Utilizing their expressions of faith can be transformational in the worship life of your church.

A word of caution: everyone thinks his or her song is great! In the coming years, churches will need to be prepared to equip and train people in this area through one-on-one mentoring, private lessons, and formal education. Christian songwriting conferences, taught by some of the best, are now common and easily accessible. Opportunities to pursue a college degree in this subject area are now readily available. More importantly, worship leaders need to understand how to integrate original songs into the church's worship repertoire while balancing issues of quality and relevance.

AVOID THE LABELS

Terms such as *contemporary, traditional,* and *blended* have limited meaning in our modern worship culture. These labels, the lightning rods for much of the musical style wars over the past 30 years, are unhelpful at best and inflammatory at worse. After all, can anyone really describe what a "contemporary" service looks like?

In truth, we all have style preferences . . . even preachers and worship leaders. We must be careful that our actions or words, or lack thereof, do not elevate a specific musical style as superior. After all, is a worship leader singing the latest Tomlin hit any more passionate than a choir singing a choral classic such as "The Majesty and Glory of Your Name"? Or, is a drummer really more energetic than an organist who plays with excellence and love of Christ? As leaders we must carefully avoid assigning adjectives to certain styles simply because we do not like them. It is unfair and egotistical and sets our congregations up for conflict.

In our various roles, the authors have the privilege of worshipping in many churches representing a wide range of stylistic approaches. Ultimately, the question is not about style but rather is the worship filled with passion, warmth, and life. Many services are nothing more than performance-oriented concerts lacking vitality and life.

Unfortunately, lack of vitality and life exists in all settings regardless of stylistic approaches. When attending these churches, one senses a lack of participation in the congregation as if people were coming to a concert hall for a rock concert or to watch a great band. In the end, empty worship is ineffective regardless of the stylistic approach. Focus on selecting the best music possible and lead it with passion and excellence. The labels serve no kingdom purpose.

LEARN THEIR MUSICAL LANGUAGE

So is musical style even an issue? The answer is yes. As worshippers it forms the basis of our worship language, the tool we use to commune and dialogue with God. If you've ever traveled in a foreign country, you understand the frustration of not being able to speak the language. The inability to communicate creates difficulties in ordering food, getting directions, or even finding a restroom. It can be a frustrating experience that leaves us feeling vulnerable and isolated from what is going on around us. Being able to speak the language is important.

This communication gap explains much of the frustration expressed during the musical style conflicts of the past 30 years. Many longtime Christians lived their lives speaking a primary worship language only to arrive one Sunday to find they are now foreigners in their own church. Their ability to communicate has been taken away. Likewise, a new believer with no church background struggles to see relevance in a language they've never heard. After all, when was the last time you heard an organ on the radio?

While no perfect strategy exists for navigating worship language differences, there are three things you can do to help make it easier. By planning services with (1) balance, (2) authenticity, and (3) excellence, churches can expand their worship repertoire to levels that age-segregated worship would never allow.

Balance involves using a wide range of elements (i.e., songs, media, instruments) that facilitate worship for different segments of the congregation. This is more about content than style. In fact, recent research conducted by the Barna Group indicated that 41 percent of millennials with a Christian background actually desire a more traditional faith rather than a hip version of it. We must never pursue cool and trendy at the expense of substance and depth. Balance is an important key.

Authenticity, or genuineness, means that people get what they see. In its truest sense, it simply implies that you are real. For example, is the way you present yourself believable to the congregation? Do the musicians come across as actually believing the words they're singing? Are the instruments a good fit for the musical style? Does the song work or is it forced? If our worship times come across as contrived, they will not connect with those seated in our churches each week. Most important, we as worship leaders must lead from the overflow of our personal walk with the Lord. We cannot take people to a place we've never been. When we try, people see right through us and our credibility is destroyed.

Finally, most people will enthusiastically embrace new elements if they are introduced with a high degree of *excellence*. Derric Johnson, the founder of Voices of Liberty at Disney's Epcot Center, has said, "We serve an excellent God and we should do so in an excellent manner." Notice we encourage excellence, not perfection. As worship leaders this distinction is important. The standard, as illustrated in Mark 12:41–44, is that we give the very best we have.

> Sitting across from the temple treasury, He watched how the crowd dropped money into the treasury. Many rich people were putting in large sums. And a poor widow came and dropped in two tiny coins worth very little. Summoning His disciples, He said to them, "I assure you: This poor widow has put in more than all those giving to the temple treasury. For they all gave out of their surplus, but she out of her poverty has put in everything she possessed—all she had to live on."

This is an important concept to grasp because skill levels vary greatly from among churches. In fact, what might be described as excellent in one setting might be mediocre in another. This can be a source of conflict when expectations are not realistically based on actual skill levels. As leaders we should demand the best from our teams, while understanding their musical limitations, and then consistently expand their skill sets toward higher levels of excellence.

GIVE CREATIVE ATTENTION TO ALL WORSHIP MUSIC

One of the primary arguments used against hymns is that they are boring.

Unfortunately, this charge is often true, not because of the hymn's content or theology, but due to uninspired and noncreative presentation. There's only one thing more boring than four stanzas of "Set My Soul Afire" sung as dirge, and that's 15 repetitions of "I Could Sing of Your Love Forever" leaving the congregation to think we are taking the song literally! The biggest obstacles we face in planning engaging worship times are worship leaders who do not take the time to plan creative approaches to the music used in worship.

DEVELOP A 1 CORINTHIANS 12 ATTITUDE— UNITY IN DIVERSITY

The importance of unity and diversity within the body of Christ are central themes throughout Scripture. The Apostle Paul reminded us of this in 1 Corinthians 12:12–14 (NIV):

> Just as a body, though one, has many parts, but all its many parts form one body, so it is with Christ. For we were all baptized by one Spirit so as to form one body—whether Jews or Gentiles, slave or free—and we were all given the one Spirit to drink. Even so the body is not made up of one part but of many.

While this passage teaches specifically on spiritual gifts, it has significant implications on the importance of pursuing unity in the midst of diversity. Most churches are comprised of multiple generations, each with different preferences and spiritual gifts. Scripture teaches us this is a good thing: the body needs all parts to be healthy. To achieve this, however, we must take on character traits of Christ, such as humility and placing the needs of others above our own, traits glaringly absent in most worship discussions. In practice, many churches are filled with immature Christians of all ages with no connection to the larger body of Christ. These folks are more than happy to be supportive as long as you sing the songs they prefer in a service of like-minded worshippers, but they are unwilling to place their own preferences aside in order to achieve the biblical mandate of unity. Sadly, some are willing to "cut off an arm" of the body of Christ simply because of differences in musical tastes!

REMEMBER, THIS IS A PROCESS, NOT AN EVENT

One of the biggest obstacles to multigenerational worship is a lack of understanding of why it is important. Church leaders must develop a strategy for intentionally discipling congregations in their journey to understanding the value of a unified worship voice. We must also control the rate of change. It is generally not change itself that causes stress, but the rate of change. When we make changes too quickly without bringing people along in their understanding of why the changes are needed, the results are generally not good. Remember, change is a process, not an event.

CONCLUSION

In Ephesians 4:14–16, Paul sums up the importance of the body of Christ being unified in the midst of the diversity:

> Then we will no longer be infants, tossed back and forth by the waves, and blown here and there by every wind of teaching and by the cunning and craftiness of people in their deceitful scheming. Instead, speaking the truth in love, we will grow to become in every respect the mature body of him who is the head, that is, Christ. From him the whole body, joined and held together by every supporting ligament, grows and builds itself up in love, as each part does its work.

As worship leaders we must work hard to keep our church families worshipping together, learning from and teaching one another. At all costs, we must avoid promoting chronological snobbery within the family by adopting a worship approach based on musical preferences. Our recommendation:

young adults need to grow up and senior adults need to get over it! We are instructed to be unified, and that must begin with corporate worship. It is when we are together, unified in the worship of our Lord, that we will find the body of Christ is strongest and most effective.

CHAPTER 3

The American Idol Experience:

PERFORMANCE-DRIVEN WORSHIP

The lights come on . . . cameras are rolling . . . the judges are in place. The singer, dressed as though he just popped off the cover of *GQ* or *Rolling Stone*, confidently steps into the spotlight at center stage. With smoke filling the air, the band begins the introduction as the featured singer adjusts his headset microphone and in-ear monitor. Large screens project the singer's image as adoring fans stand and cheer his performance.

Downtown is a completely different setting. Singers enter the choir loft in the almost gothic cathedral, fully adorned in robes and carrying folders filled with anthems representing the best in choral literature. As the majestic pipe organ sounds out the opening measures of "A Mighty Fortress Is Our God," the minister of music, dressed in a tailored suit, prepares to lead the singers in the call to worship. Television cameras capture every move as adoring fans quietly sit and cheer on their performance.

Welcome to Sunday mornings in America. In June 2002, American television audiences were introduced to *American Idol*, which became one of the most successful shows in history. Each week on the show viewers follow contestants on their journey to become the "next American idol." The contestants hope to duplicate the success of Kelly Clarkson, Jennifer Hudson, or Carrie Underwood. Viewers choose the ultimate winner through telephone, online, and text message voting. Every year more than 100,000 people line up for auditions in cities across the country, looking for the magic golden ticket to Hollywood!

The success of *American Idol* led the way for other reality-based shows including *The Voice*, *America's Got Talent*, and *The X Factor*. With such a huge fan base, it was only a matter of time before a "baptized" version appeared. *Gifted*, produced in 2007 by Trinity Broadcasting Network, featured famous Christian artists as guest hosts and judges, including Stryper lead singer Michael Sweet and Brian Littrell of Backstreet Boys. The grand prize winner received a major recording contract with EMI Christian Music Group. While 16,000 contestants auditioned for *Gifted,* it was canceled after one season. We can debate the wisdom of this copycat effort, but one thing is crystal clear: many people want to be stars!

The Contemporary Christian Music (CCM) industry keeps that dream alive for many aspiring musicians. With its origins in the Jesus movement during the late 1960s and 1970s, the CCM industry exploded into an economic titan with sales of more than 23 million units in 2012. With dozens of genres and categories, ranging from hip-hop to Christian punk and Southern gospel to pop/contemporary, the industry holds its own nationally televised awards show, the *Dove Awards*, annually in Nashville, Tennessee. Sponsored by the Gospel Music Association (GMA), musicians annually receive awards in various categories including Male Vocalist of the Year, Artist of the Year, and Group of the Year, categories strikingly similar to those found in the secular music industry.

Like secular artists, Christian artists and their bands load rented buses with rented equipment and head out on regional or national tours to promote their latest album, expand their fan base, and generate revenue from product sales. These events attract thousands of concert goers, with ticket prices ranging from free to more than $50 per person. Christian promoters work with performance halls, churches, and college campuses to host concerts. The goal is making a profit. With rising production costs and a volatile economy, margins are small, but the allure of fame and fortune keep the industry growing.

More than 1,000 Christian radio stations across the country support the CCM industry. K-LOVE radio, one example, boasts nearly 12 million listeners weekly. Through a series of independent stations and transmitters, K-LOVE radio programming is simulcast to 446 signals in 47 states. Stations like K-LOVE exert an enormous influence on the CCM world and can make or break the career of an aspiring artist.

Although first and foremost a business, the industry is populated with Christian artists with a sincere heart for ministry. Many artists are actively involved in social ministry or missions-related organizations, in addition to regular concerts. In 2013, CCM artist Natalie Grant narrated and produced *In Plain Sight: Stories of Hope and Freedom*, a film seeking to raise awareness for women and children forced into the commercial sex trade each year in the United States. Other artists champion social concerns such as adoption, homelessness, hunger, and clean drinking water for third-world countries. These are excellent examples of how artists leverage their renown to prompt their fans to action. Since many fans are millennials, members of a generation with a deep passion for social issues, they respond.

The CCM industry and its artists are naturally a part of the fabric of the local church. Not only are Christians their target market but most CCM industry executives and artists chose this path because of their faith. In recent years, this connection with local churches has grown stronger as a growing number of artists, such as Charles Billingsley, Mark Harris, Kristian Stanfill, and Travis Cottrell, joined church staffs in roles as worship leaders and songwriters. In these roles, artists partner with a community of believers and keep their concert ministries framed within a ministry context. These roles also provide consistent income for these artists in an industry where long-term success can, at best, be elusive.

Christian artists make a significant contribution to the lives of believers. Their ministries encourage us and bring positive, faith-based entertainment to our lives. The CCM industry provides the modern church with an infusion of fresh song literature and served as a stimulus for worship renewal over the past three decades. The problem arises when the lines between performer and worshipper are not defined. While both roles serve a function, the ability to distinguish the two is critical. Many seem unable to do this.

IT'S NOT JUST CCM

Worship leaders in more traditional churches with choirs and orchestras are also guilty of pursuing the "star factor." Though difficult at times to distinguish between concerts and modern worship services, many traditional choirs in more formal worship services are just as performance-driven as the rock-and-roll church down the street. If the focus is on the music or individuals, it does not matter whether it's a singer with a guitar or an organist with an attitude. The results are the same: performance-driven worship.

Performance-driven worship has influenced those sitting in the pew. While the *American Idol* judges may have a revolving door, our churches are filled with people who have no problem filling the role of judge. They arrive each week, take their seat in the judge's chair, and proceed to evaluate every aspect of the "program" for that day. Their standards often include stylistic preference, song choice, and musical quantity. The folks in the pew know how to fulfill the role of judge. After a decade of watching reality-based talent shows, church members actually know when the performance is good and when it is not. Using descriptions such as "pitchy" and "poor song choice," church members offer their critiques as if they were Simon Cowell himself!

 ## A BIBLICAL RESPONSE

The major problem with performance-driven worship is that the congregation is robbed of the opportunity to respond directly to God. Though the lyrics may be about God, or even directed to God, placing the focus on individuals ends the opportunity for worship. The music may be excellent and move people emotionally, but if not correctly focused, it is nothing more than entertainment. As worship leaders, we are to help people direct, or at times redirect, their attention and affection to the right Person. While it sounds simple, it is not. Leading authentic worship is like walking a spiritual tightrope while balancing musical excellence, passion, and humility. If the leader leans too far in either direction, the entire experience crashes.

Worship, in its most basic form, is a dialogue with God, a conversation He initiates with us. If you ever tried to have a conversation with someone who is nonresponsive, you understand what is missing when the response of the people is taken away. Because God desires communion with us, He initiates a dialogue by revealing Himself through Scripture, music, prayer, or preaching. The dialogue, however, is cut short, or may never start, because worship leaders allow the people's response to come to them.

Isaiah 6 provides a beautiful example of how this dialogue should work. Isaiah is engaged in an intense dialogue with God, a dialogue accented by a pattern of revelation-response found throughout Scripture. In examining this passage, we find elements of worship that serve as responses to God's revelation.

THE PATTERN OF REVELATION-RESPONSE

ISAIAH 6:1–9

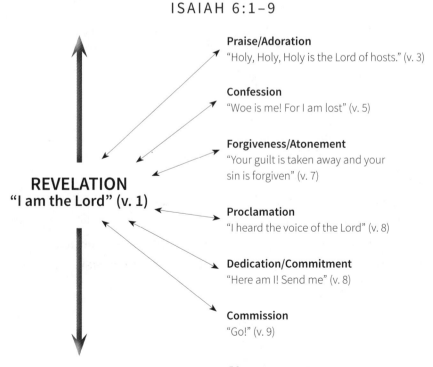

REVELATION
"I am the Lord" (v. 1)

Praise/Adoration
"Holy, Holy, Holy is the Lord of hosts." (v. 3)

Confession
"Woe is me! For I am lost" (v. 5)

Forgiveness/Atonement
"Your guilt is taken away and your sin is forgiven" (v. 7)

Proclamation
"I heard the voice of the Lord" (v. 8)

Dedication/Commitment
"Here am I! Send me" (v. 8)

Commission
"Go!" (v. 9)

Note the element of *revelation* is different than the others for two important reasons. First, *revelation* is the work of God Himself and cannot be controlled by us. Secondly, revelation runs throughout the worship experience and serves as the basis of our different responses.

As church leaders we often are guilty of trying to create worship. In reality, we can manipulate emotions with song choices, lighting, and spoken words, but we cannot manufacture worship. God always initiates the encounter; we cannot create it.

- When God revealed Himself to Adam in the garden of Eden, it was at His initiation.
- When God revealed Himself to Noah to give instructions on the building of the ark, it was at His initiation.
- When God revealed Himself to Abraham to make His covenant, it was at His initiation.
- When God revealed Himself to Moses in the form of a burning bush, it was at His initiation.
- When Jesus revealed Himself to Paul on the road to Damascus, it was at His initiation.
- When Jesus revealed Himself to John on the Isle of Patmos, it was at His initiation.
- When God reveals Himself to us, it is at His initiation!

𝄢 WHAT NOW?

How do we avoid becoming performers instead of facilitators of worship? Can we even present music with excellence and yet redirect the focus to God? Can the trappings of the Christian artist be successfully integrated into local church settings? Is it possible to get congregations out of their judge's seat and into a God-centered dialogue? Church leaders will face these important questions in the upcoming years as they assess the influence of performance on church worship experiences. Here are several suggestions to help guide those efforts.

WE ARE MINISTERS FIRST, MUSICIANS SECOND

The importance of worship leaders having a clear and definite call to ministry has taken a backseat as churches have become more entertainment-driven. For many years the first order of business was to determine a candidate's call to ministry and his personal walk with God. Over time, as the focus shifted to musical talent and technological skills, confirmation of a call to ministry often never enters the conversation. The simple question, What has God called you to do? should be the starting point for any potential worship pastor. How we view that calling by God influences everything in our lives. It impacts:

- How we relate to our senior pastor.
- How we deal with church members.
- How we relate to other staff members.
- How we work with our music and worship leaders.
- How we view the relationship with our families.
- It will be the single most important factor that keeps you in the ministry when things get tough . . . and they will get tough.

The problem is augmented by the fact that many pastors and church leaders view staff as employees or contract workers. The titles used in many churches transfer the focus from pastoral responsibilities to musical function. Many no longer refer to those facilitating worship as ministers or pastors but simply as leaders or assistants. These shifts have huge theological implications.

While the role of worship leader is not a biblical office, those of pastor and teacher are. Ephesians 4:11–13 identifies these offices:

> *And He personally gave some to be apostles, some prophets, some evangelists, some pastors and teachers, for the training of the saints in the work of ministry, to build up the body of Christ, until we all reach unity in the faith and in the knowledge of God's Son, growing into a mature man with a stature measured by Christ's fullness.*

This passage outlines important responsibilities in our roles as pastors and teachers. *Pastor*, from the Greek word *poimein* means "shepherd," a major function of those leading worship ministries. Worship leaders shepherd and teach their singers, instrumentalists, and technical teams. In doing this, worship leaders exercise leadership, discipleship, and ministry, important responsibilities central to their calling as ministers of the gospel.

Many problems associated with performance-driven worship can be eliminated if churches focus on securing men and women who are called, rather than simply skilled, to fill ministry positions. Backgrounds, qualifications, education, and experience, while important, do not qualify us to be ministers. Only God's call qualifies you as a minister of the gospel. It was John Newton, the famous English pastor and author of "Amazing Grace," who stated, "None but He who made the world can make a Minister of the Gospel."

Churches constructing job descriptions for worship leaders must begin with the spiritual requirements God outlined in His Word:

> This saying is trustworthy: "If anyone aspires to be an overseer, he desires a noble work." An overseer, therefore, must be above reproach, the husband of one wife, self-controlled, sensible, respectable, hospitable, an able teacher, not addicted to wine, not a bully but gentle, not quarrelsome, not greedy—one who manages his own household competently, having his children under control with all dignity. (If anyone does not know how to manage his own household, how will he take care of God's church?) He must not be a new convert, or he might become conceited and fall into the condemnation of the Devil. Furthermore, he must have a good reputation among outsiders, so that he does not fall into disgrace and the Devil's trap.
> (1 Timothy 3:1–7)

IT'S A HEART ISSUE

Worship rather than performance is a matter of the heart. Worship pastors must lead from the overflow of our personal journey with the Lord. David, a skillful musician in his own right, was a "man after God's own heart." He certainly was not perfect and made bad decisions and had moral failures and suffered the consequences of those, but his passion as a worshipper and pursuer of God, rather than his mistakes, defined his life. So how do you pursue a heart like God's?

A PASSION FOR GOD'S WORD

As Christians, and specifically as worship leaders, a passion for God's Word is foundational. We spend significant time developing our musical skills, preparing for worship times, and doing "church" things, often at the exclusion of studying and absorbing God's Word. If you are honest with yourself, the problem is obvious. Since we generally spend more time being musicians than pursuing God, our lives are out of balance. To correct our personal course, we must recalibrate through shifting our priorities and focus. While our journey with Christ should not be comprised of meaningless ritual, that journey must be intentional and systematic.

There really is no excuse for failure. Christian bookstore shelves are loaded with resources and devotional guides. One may find significant Bible study resources on the Internet. It is up to us to make the commitment to spend time with Him every day in study and prayer . . . and then follow through! If our spirits are dry and parched, musicians will revert to their musical skills resulting in empty performances where worship should abound.

A PASSION FOR GOD'S PRESENCE

While we spend most of our time preparing for worship "events," many have lost their passion for God to reveal Himself through these events. We are passionate about the music, not His presence. In fact, what would we do if God literally showed up?

God has done just that—shown up! In fact, every biblical account of God's revelation is followed by a passionate, emotional, and life-changing response from His people. One of the most spectacular was the dedication of Solomon's temple in 2 Chronicles 7:1–3 (NIV):

> When Solomon finished praying, fire came down from heaven and consumed the burnt offering and the sacrifices, and the glory of the LORD filled the temple. The priests could not enter the temple of the LORD because the glory of the LORD filled it. When all the Israelites saw the fire coming down and the glory of the LORD above the temple, they knelt on the pavement with their faces to the ground, and they worshiped and gave thanks to the LORD, saying, "He is good; his love endures forever."

Do you remember the last time "fire came down from heaven" in your life? How long has it been since God's presence was so heavy and thick as you led in worship that you could hardly breathe?

While we desire our churches to experience this type of power, we cannot take people to a place we have not been. Just as preachers spend time studying and internalizing their sermon content, worship leaders should do the same. This can include using the service music for the upcoming week as part of your daily time with the Lord. This allows the lyrics to become part of who you are. Then, when we stand before our people, we are not reading unfamiliar words on the teleprompter. The words have been part of our personal worship the entire week. When we lead worship with passion exhibiting the presence of God in our lives, we are less likely to be mere performers.

A PASSION FOR GOD'S PEOPLE

Someone quipped, "Ministry would be great if it weren't for the people." If you have served a church for as few as 24 hours, you understand the intent of that statement: working with people is hard! Since people have an emotional connection with music, worship leaders are often the object of complaints and grumbling. In a given week we received complaints that the music was too traditional *and* too contemporary—about the same service!

While our emotional first response is to pull a page from the wrestling world and body-slam the complainer(s), God has a better idea.

We are called to love! This is difficult, since you may be the target of negative comments, anonymous letters, or personal attacks. It helps if you view the people in your ministry as gifts, even those who hurtful, make personal and offensive remarks, and take unkind action. When we focus on loving those God entrusted to us, our perspective and the manner in which we lead worship changes.

A PASSION FOR GOD'S PURPOSE

Do we have a passion to see God's purposes realized in the lives of the people we lead, or is our position simply a platform for accomplishing our own goals? Pursuit of God's plan and purposes impacts all areas of our ministry.

- Is the planned recording project important for our church, or is it something to place another professional notch in our belt?
- Is the song we wrote last week really what the church needs, or are we too involved in the artistic endeavor to be objective?
- Are the songs we use based on my preferences or where the church is musically and spiritually?
- When I make statements such as, "Style is not important," am I actually saying, "Your style is not important?"

This list goes on *ad infinitum*, but the message is clear. We must passionately pursue God's purposes and plans for His people, not our own. When we pursue God, all our activities (calendars, events, worship services) become about accomplishing His purposes rather than about leading successful events to pad our musical résumés.

UNDERSTAND THE ROLES

Performance-driven worship often results from faulty understanding of our roles in worship. Danish theologian Søren Kierkegaard's (1813–55) worship model warrants a quick review. Kierkegaard's model compares worship to a drama in which worship leaders serve as actors and God is the prompter who gives cues to the leaders instructing them what to do next. The congregation takes on the role of audience or, most often, the panel of judges. The problem with this model is we are in the wrong roles. In biblical worship those seated in our congregations are the actors, the persons leading worship are the prompters, and God becomes an Audience of One. What would happen if we actually adopted this model? I know we talk about it and say we believe it, but can you image the impact of a church that actually did this?

If worship leaders could instill this one understanding in their teams, it would revolutionize their impact for the kingdom. Unfortunately, we often send conflicting messages. The minute we refer to the platform as a "stage," we place ourselves in the role of actor, or performer, and elevate those we lead into a role reserved for God: the audience. When preachers or worship leaders talk about the "stage," it reinforces our inaccurate understanding of our roles in worship and screams a lack of theological understanding. There is no stage . . . we are not performers . . . God is the audience!

LET THE PEOPLE RESPOND

How can we, as worship leaders, encourage our people to respond to God's revelation? Scripture is filled with examples of appropriate responses ranging from singing (more than 85 references) to dancing before the Lord. We must resist dictating how people respond. Instead, we must create an atmosphere of freedom that allows authentic interaction with God.

SINGING

♩= **1 Chronicles 16:23**—"Sing to the LORD, all the earth. Proclaim His salvation from day to day."

♩= **Psalm 30:11–12**—"You turned my lament into dancing; You removed my sackcloth and clothed me with gladness, so that I can sing to You and not be silent. Lord my God, I will praise You forever."

♩= **Psalm 92:1–3**—"It is good to praise Yahweh, to sing praise to Your name, Most High, to declare Your faithful love in the morning and Your faithfulness at night, with a ten-stringed harp and the music of a lyre."

♩= **Psalm 100:2**—"Serve the Lᴏʀᴅ with gladness; come before Him with joyful songs."

♩= **Colossians 3:16**—"Let the message about the Messiah dwell richly among you, teaching and admonishing one another in all wisdom, and singing psalms, hymns, and spiritual songs, with gratitude in your hearts to God."

♩= **James 5:13**—"Is anyone among you suffering? He should pray. Is anyone cheerful? He should sing praises."

♩= **Ephesians 5:19–21**—"Speak to one another in psalms, hymns, and spiritual songs, singing and making music from your heart to the Lord, giving thanks always for everything to God the Father in the name of our Lord Jesus Christ, submitting to one another in the fear of Christ."

PRAYER

♩= **Ephesians 6:18**—"Pray at all times in the Spirit with every prayer and request, and stay alert in this with all perseverance and intercession for all the saints."

♩= **1 Corinthians 14:15**—"What then? I will pray with the spirit, and I will also pray with my understanding. I will sing with the spirit, and I will also sing with my understanding."

♩= **1 Timothy 2:1–2**—"First of all, then, I urge that petitions, prayers, intercessions, and thanksgivings be made for everyone, for kings and all those who are in authority, so that we may lead a tranquil and quiet life in all godliness and dignity."

GREETING EACH OTHER

♩= **Romans 16:16**—"Greet one another with a holy kiss. All the churches of Christ send you greetings."

♪= **1 Peter 5:14**—"Greet one another with a kiss of love. Peace to all of you who are in Christ."

LIFTING UP OF HANDS

♪= **Psalm 63:4**—"So I will praise You as long as I live; at Your name, I will lift up my hands."

♪= **Psalm 134:2**—"Lift up your hands in the holy place and praise the LORD!"

♪= **1 Timothy 2:8**—"Therefore, I want the men in every place to pray, lifting up holy hands without anger or argument."

♪= **Psalm 141:2**—"May my prayer be set before You as incense, the raising of my hands as the evening offering."

KNEELING

♪= **Psalm 95:6**—"Come, let us worship and bow down; let us kneel before the LORD our Maker."

♪= **Luke 22:41–42**—"Then He withdrew from them about a stone's throw, knelt down, and began to pray, 'Father, if You are willing, take this cup away from Me—nevertheless, not My will, but Yours, be done.'"

DANCING

♪= **Psalm 149:3**—"Let them praise His name with dancing and make music to Him with tambourine and lyre."

♪= **Psalm 150:4**—"Praise Him with tambourine and dance; praise Him with flute and strings."

♪= **2 Samuel 6:14–15**—"David was dancing with all his might before the LORD wearing a linen ephod. He and the whole house of Israel were bringing up the ark of the LORD with shouts and the sound of the ram's horn."

CLAPPING

♩= **Psalm 47:1**—"Clap your hands, all you peoples; shout to God with a jubilant cry."

SHOUTING

♩=**Psalm 95:1–2**—"Come, let us shout joyfully to the LORD, shout triumphantly to the rock of our salvation! Let us enter His presence with thanksgiving; let us shout triumphantly to Him in song."

CONCLUSION

Performance-driven worship, while not new, has grown to epidemic proportions in the modern church. Throughout the twentieth century, evangelistic singers such as Homer Rodeheaver, George Beverly Shea, and Doug Oldham were popular with crusade and church congregations across the United States and served as early examples of Christian artists. The rise of the CCM industry in the 1970s, however, gave voice to a new generation of musicians seeking to express their musical and professional ambitions in the area of performance and recording, thus propelling Christian artists to a new level. While the concept was not new, singers such as Bill Gaither, Sandi Patty, and Michael W. Smith leveraged the role into fame and financial success. By 1990, the lines between church and concert began to blur as popular Christian music was infused into local church worship. Many worship leaders attempted to duplicate the appeal of CCM artists on Sunday mornings, creating concert events using the latest technological advances and musical offerings available to the industry.

Running parallel to developments in the CCM industry was a focus on performance in more formal church settings. For decades, many established churches utilized choirs, orchestras, and highly trained singers in musical presentations that rivaled the finest concert halls in the United States. As media technology advanced through the 1990s, many churches offered television broadcasts to reach more people. While some broadcasts originated from megachurches with thousands of members, most originated locally using cable-access or regional stations. In all cases, the pastors and worship leaders achieved celebrity status, if only in their own communities. With television came more focus on standards of quality and presentation, which pushed the expectations even higher.

Though the two streams used differing approaches, they were unified by one characteristic: performance. To a large part, churches of all sizes, locations, and methodologies bought into a performance-driven worship model. As churches struggle with the influence of consumerism and rise of the church shopper, pressure to meet quality and style demands resulted in an increased emphasis on platform personalities and effectively devalued the role of the congregation. In a reversion to a pre-Reformation era, we have taken the work of the people and given it back to performers.

Over the next ten years churches will continue to integrate Christian artists into the fabric of local church life. With the changing and, at times, diminishing role of choirs and symphonic orchestras, church identities will be decidedly less traditional as millennials continue to move into adulthood. With about 61 percent of the population under the age of 45, according to the 2010 census, the worship language must continue to shift to be relevant, while trying to balance stylistic demands of an aging buster and boomer generation. This new generation of young artists and worship leaders will struggle with finding balance, but their creativity and passion for evangelism will serve churches well.

Performance-driven worship has taken its toll on churches. Most struggle to define the boundaries that separate entertainment and worship. This is not *American Idol*! Church members need to step out of the judge's chair and cease focusing on individual preferences, likes, and dislikes. Likewise, it is time for worship leaders to step out of the spotlight. When it comes to worship, it was never intended for us.

CHAPTER 4

The Worship Mirage:

TRAINING WORSHIP LEADERS TO LEAD CHURCHES THAT DON'T EXIST

mi·rage [mə-rahzh]—*something illusory: something that appears to be real but is unreal or merely imagined*

Mirages, optical illusions caused by the refraction of light rays in the atmosphere, cause people to see things that do not exist. A famous example is the discovery of Crocker Land in 1818 by British explorers John and James Ross. Searching to find a passage between the Atlantic and Pacific Oceans, the Ross brothers gave up when they determined mountains blocked the way. In 1906, American polar explorer Robert Peary confirmed their discovery when he reported, "We saw the mountains and called them Crocker Land." There was a problem, however. These mountains simply did not exist.

In 1913, the American Museum of Natural History commissioned Donald B. MacMillan to lead an expedition to find the elusive land mass. After searching the Arctic for several weeks, MacMillan reported the following, as reported by the *New York Times* in 1915:

> Crocker Land, reported seen by Peary in 1906, and indicated on the latest maps, does not exist. I succeeded in

covering the whole distance of 1,200 miles in seventy-two days. To us, standing on the heights of Cape Thomas Hubbard, and for several days on the polar sea, there was every appearance of an immense tract of land extending along 120 degrees of the horizon, hills, valley and snow-capped peaks.

Further travel toward the northwest caused it to change its direction with the revolving of the sun. It constantly varied in extent and character and finally on our last march disappeared entirely.

How does this relate to worship education? As worship culture made monumental shifts, colleges and seminaries dismissed the changes as passing fads or trends. While churches adopted modern expressions of worship, educational institutions continued teaching traditional approaches, often ignoring the changes taking place. A chasm developed between educators and local church practitioners. Demonstrating musical snobbery and elitism, each side championed the superiority of its approach. Each year, as graduates accepted church positions, it became increasingly clear they were ill-equipped to handle actual job demands. Colleges and seminaries worked hard to train students, but they prepared them to serve churches that no longer existed using approaches as effective as traveling toward an arctic mirage.

By the end of the twentieth century, many church leaders viewed formal music education as irrelevant to the modern worship movement. The result was declining enrollment, increased tension between academics and practitioners, and a diminished influence on a new generation of worship leaders. Since the 1940s, earning a seminary music degree had been a prerequisite for church musicians. Now it was a detriment.

EARLY DEVELOPMENTS (1945–66)

Following World War II, many veterans returned home with renewed religious vigor and a new desire to live out their faith. Churches responded by creating new ministry positions, including roles for song leaders and choir directors. Although larger churches had employed full-time ministers of music, paid church positions became more common. Seminaries and Christian colleges began offering church music degrees designed to develop traditional music skills (i.e., conducting, voice, organ, and piano) in this new crop of church musicians. After graduating, these leaders assumed church positions and helped shape a worship model based on a classical style, a model largely unchallenged by Southern Baptists and other mainline churches through the mid-1960s.

This found fertile ground in a church environment in which there was a clearly defined, somewhat monolithic church program structure of missions education and mission support. Virtually all churches did the same thing every week. While sermons varied greatly as there was no subscribed sermon series, educational offerings were fairly similar across the board.

WINDS OF CHANGE (1967–90)

The changes in worship culture between 1967 and 1990 are best understood as the sum of independent forces, each having their own trajectories then converging to produce something unique: the Praise and Worship movement.

> Arguably the single biggest alteration in the life of the average evangelical congregation within the last 30 years has been the sweeping change in the music that is played on Sunday morning. Where organ and piano, formal choirs, and vocal soloists and groups once held sway over a slowly-changing canon of staid hymnody and peppy gospel songs, a flood of guitars and "praise choruses" suddenly came rushing in during the 1970s. An irresistible, grassroots, pop-culture-driven force met the immovable object of tradition and sentiment, and the ensuing years saw no shortage of conflict and controversy as a result.[1]

To appreciate the diversity of these forces, it helps to briefly look at three individually. Though other influences existed, including the growing prominence of media (television, radio) and reforms of the Second Vatican Council (1962–65), the central contributions came from the Jesus movement, the youth musical movement, and the rise of contemporary Christian music.

JESUS MOVEMENT

Historians identify the 1960s as one of the most turbulent eras in American history. This decade, accented by assassinations, civil unrest, and a nation engaged in an unpopular war in Vietnam, gave rise to one of the most influential movements in modern Christianity, the Jesus movement. *The Hollywood Free Paper* (hollywoodfreepaper.org) observes in "A Brief History of the Jesus Movement":

> In many ways the spring and summer of 1967 was a bleak moment in America. Three astronauts were killed in the Apollo 1 explosion, and in Vietnam, American troops were moving into the Mekong Delta, and massing along the Cambodian border. Antiwar protests were escalating alongside the war itself, with draft card burnings, marches and other forms of demonstration on the rise. Black unrest was smoldering in cities across the nation in the wake of the Watts riots two years earlier.

Initiated on the West Coast, communal communities of faith targeting the hippie culture spread across the United States and spawned innovations in worship that continue to reverberate.

As the number of so-called Jesus People grew, it was only a matter of time before their influence was felt in the established church. One of the early centers to embrace the movement was Pastor Chuck Smith and Calvary Chapel in Costa Mesa, California. Smith encouraged young musicians to use their talents to share Christ and led Calvary Chapel to introduce an informal and contemporary approach to its worship and public meetings.

Under Smith's leadership, Calvary Chapel enlisted Lonnie Frisbee, a "young hippie," as a missionary to the youth of Orange County. Larry Eskridge notes Frisbee's impact on the community was immediate: "By the middle of 1968, the church was filling up with barefoot, blue-jean-wearing kids, and dozens of hippies and teenage runaways inhabited a string of communal homes sponsored by Calvary Chapel with names like the House of Miracles and Mansion Messiah." The influence of Calvary Chapel was immense. In addition to their pioneering efforts in evangelism to the era's youth subculture, much of contemporary Christian music (CCM) has its roots in Calvary Chapel worship music.

YOUTH MUSICAL MOVEMENT

Beginning in the mid-1960s, church leaders began to understand music's potential to reach youth for Christ. While some churches had youth choirs, the literature was almost exclusively traditional. State Baptist conventions in Mississippi, Texas, and Georgia commonly sponsored mass youth choir festivals featuring classical oratorios such as Mendelssohn's *Elijah* and Handel's *Messiah*. When the youth choir musical *Good News* was published in 1967, everything changed.

Good News, the brainchild of Billy Ray Hearn — minister of music at First Baptist Church, Thomasville, Georgia — Cecil McGee, and Bob Oldenburg, was published by the Recreation Department of the Baptist Sunday School Board in Nashville, Tennessee. The musical premiered that year at Glorieta Baptist Assembly in New Mexico and Ridgecrest Baptist Assembly in North Carolina. A presentation at the 1968 Southern Baptist Convention in Houston, Texas, featuring 1,300 students and a 50-piece orchestra, propelled the sale of an estimated 2 million copies of the musical and launched a youth choir movement in churches across the nation.

The success of *Good News*, both in economic terms and local church appeal, led to a steady stream of youth musicals. These works included

Tell It Like It Is (1968), which included the song "Pass It On," and *Celebrate Life* (1972), featuring the communion-themed song "In Remembrance." Denominational hymnals later included both songs, indicating their acceptance across congregations.

Interestingly, among Southern Baptists, 1972 was the zenith in baptisms. Peaking at 445,725, baptisms by and large continued to decline until the present time in which we are down to levels that match 1948.

CONTEMPORARY CHRISTIAN MUSIC

The music of the Jesus movement, often referred to as Jesus Rock, focused on evangelism, apologetics, and entertainment. Drawing heavily on folk music, the songs were deeply emotional and served as tools for evangelistic outreach. Elmer L. Towns and Vernon M. Whaley write, in *Worship Through the Ages: How the Great Awakenings Shape Evangelical Worship*:

> Early Jesus music reflected the commercial folk music of popular groups like the New Christy Minstrels and Peter, Paul and Mary. Heavily driven by guitar, the songs were harmonically simple and lyrically straightforward. Platform presentations were deliberately unpretentious. What emerged was a mixture of pop, folk, soft rock, country, and rock 'n' roll.

This growth in popularity and acceptance by young adult culture pioneered a new genre of music called contemporary Christian music (CCM) that would grow into a multibillion-dollar industry.

> During the 1970s, CCM radically changed the way evangelicals perceived the relationship between worship and music. For the first time in church history, worship and music were seen as synonymous. By the beginning of the 1990s, a new paradigm for worship was in place.[2]

A NEW PARADIGM

By 1990, the forces converged into what is commonly called the Praise and Worship movement. As more churches integrated this new genre into worship services, the challenge of finding ministers of music equipped to handle its unique requirements grew. Praise and worship music required expertise in technology and modern instruments, skills not taught in colleges and seminaries. Other nonmusical influences began to erode the confidence pastors had in finding trained music and worship personnel. These influences included:

- Baby boomers were middle-aged, and their children emerged as generation X.
- New technology and the Internet.
- Megachurches emerged with new opportunities for musicians.
- The seeker-sensitive or purpose-driven churches influenced growth and worship practices.[3]

Around the year 2000, the evangelical church experienced another, far-reaching paradigm shift. Change was the rule of thumb. The postmodern demand for experience, coupled with a commitment to sincerity emerged. Still, some two decades into these changes, most seminaries and Christian colleges continued to focus on traditional skills and made minimal, if any, changes to curricula. As a new millennial generation began to take center stage, pastors and church leaders, once loyal to their favorite Christian college or seminary for finding staff equipped to lead their worship, turned to other sources.

A BIBLICAL RESPONSE
HELD TO A HIGHER STANDARD

Those charged with teaching the next generation of worship leaders have an enormous responsibility, and Scripture does not take it lightly. James 3:1–2 reminds leaders, "Not many should become teachers, my brothers, knowing that we will receive a stricter judgment, for we all stumble in many ways. If anyone does not stumble in what he says, he is a mature man who is also able to control his whole body." This passage clearly teaches we will be held to a "stricter judgment" based on how we fulfill this calling. Our pursuit of the heart of God shapes how we view the world, our art, and our calling. This must not be approached lackadaisically. Worship leaders must lead from the overflow and educators should do the same.

The Great Commandment and the Great Commission serve as prisms that shape how we view our culture, our educational philosophies, and the content we teach. The price for shading truth to protect personal preference is huge; therefore, our teaching must be biblical, transparent, and truthful. The Apostle Paul affirmed these principles in 2 Timothy 2:15, "Be diligent to present yourself approved to God, a worker who doesn't need to be ashamed, correctly teaching the word of truth." The importance of these characteristics is also emphasized in Titus 2:6–8:

> In the same way, encourage the young men to be self-controlled in everything. Make yourself an example of good works with integrity and dignity in your teaching. You message is to be sound beyond reproach, so that the opponent will be ashamed, having nothing bad to say about us.

This passage highlights the importance of being a good example to those we teach. Students watch how we respond when challenged, and the millennial generation will challenge what we say. Oftentimes their questions are rhetorical and based on a search they just conducted on their computer or phone. As a result, our teaching must be "beyond reproach" and based on solid biblical understanding. Millennials abhor a lack of authenticity, so educators must demonstrate self-control, integrity, and dignity for the message to be heard. The question is not, Will you be challenged? but How will you respond when challenged?

A MINISTRY OF INFLUENCE

Teachers often are some of the most influential people in our lives. Most people can name professors in college or seminary who shaped their view of God and understanding of Scripture. This should cause Christian educators to shake in their boots. Like clay on a potter's wheel, teachers shape the way worship leaders approach ministry. What we say matters. Luke 6:40 underscores this idea: "A disciple is not above his teacher, but everyone who is fully trained will be like his teacher." Many of those who sit under our teaching will buy in to what we say and throughout their ministries our influence will indirectly impact churches, families, and individuals in unimaginable ways. Are the lessons and principles we pour into our students worthy of the calling God has placed on our lives?

𝄢 WHAT NOW?

Several years ago, a colleague was noticeably irritated after teaching a seminary class. When asked why, he responded, "I'm giving them the answers, and they don't even know the questions." For far too long church music educators have asked the wrong questions. While focused on protecting musical standards and stylistic preferences, we overlooked questions such as, Are we training students for the right market? and Is our approach even relevant to the modern church musician? Our path forward will be largely dependent on a new set of questions:

- For what purpose are we equipping students?
- Is our primary goal to equip our students for ministry or music?
- What role do local pastors have in helping us shape worship curricula?
- Are we teaching our church music and worship students to think as innovators and communicators of biblical truth?
- Why are the number of students involved in church music programs and well-respected schools of music declining?[4]

A JACK-OF-ALL-TRADES

Thirty years ago when a church began its search for a worship leader, most called a seminary or denominational office to get recommendations. In response, they received several résumés based on personality as well as academic and professional success. This was a logical approach since most church musicians were trained with identical skill sets. Likewise, most churches had similar worship identities built around either classical or gospel hymn traditions. A worship service for a Baptist church in Texas was remarkably similar to one in South Carolina: they used choirs, piano, organ, and people sang from the same hymnbook. My how things have changed!

Gone are the days of consistent church identities. Today every church has its own DNA and a specific skill-set requirement for potential worship leaders. Some use choirs and orchestra, while others use vocal teams and bands. Many churches define themselves as hip-hop, alternative, modern, cowboy, blended, contemporary . . . and the list goes on.

Expectations for the modern worship leader extend well beyond musical skills. The worship pastor is no longer just the resident staff musician. Today, the worship pastor, an equal partner in ministry, must be a theologian, pastor, counselor, mentor, producer, videographer, audio engineer, leader, and servant. The worship pastor must develop strong communication and relational skills, learn to negotiate and compromise, and understand how to analyze costs versus benefits. To meet these expectations, students called to the worship ministry must have more skills than ever before.

MODERN SKILL SETS

Over the next decade, institutions that teach broad skill sets for worship practitioners will be most successful. Those who continue to resist changing will face declining enrollment and the elimination of church music programs. So, what questions must be asked when developing curricula for the training of worship pastors as skilled practitioners? Here are a few suggestions:[5]

- What specific skills must be developed?
- What is the process for developing worship skills?
- Do we as musicians and artists teach worship theology? Is this something better left up to the "theology professors"?
- How do we equip worship pastors to handle the onslaught of innovations brought on by the information age, social media, 24-hour news, and changing technological dynamics?

- How do we teach our students to handle the barrage of technical resources needed for effective ministry?
- Is it our job to teach our students how to get along with the senior pastor, respond to the dynamics of an executive staff, or deal with the unpredictable nature of a personnel committee?
- What music skills are relevant for the modern worship leader?
- Do we continue to teach music theory based on a model shaped and canonized by the common practice period?
- Do we teach market-driven skills such as Nashville Numbers and jazz chords?
- Are we teaching our students to master dictation skills well enough to successfully do take downs off of a CD or their MP3 players?
- Do we teach students to write and compose music *the old-fashioned way*—with a pencil and sheet of manuscript paper—or do we encourage them to use their innate, play-by-ear aural abilities and computer savvy to create music using Logic Pro, Finale, or GarageBand software?
- What about management concepts such as planning processes, budget administration, negotiation, and accountability?
- How do we teach communication and relational skills?

Music schools must also transform their modes of delivery. Residential, online, blended, mentor, and satellite programs are central to the future success of church music education. Although teaching applied music (i.e., voice, guitar, drums, piano, conducting) in online format presents challenges, the fact that more than 6.1 million students were enrolled in online courses in fall 2010 makes finding solutions a priority.

THE CLASSICAL MODEL

Integrating new requirements into established educational models is difficult. Traditionally, evangelical colleges adopt one of four approaches to developing curricula and training ministers of music and worship:

- Provide students sensing a call into the worship ministry a path through a traditional music education degree.

- Provide musicians longing to serve in the church a path through a music performance degree.
- Provide students a hybrid degree path through combining a music education and professional performance degree into an interdisciplinary program that also meets accreditation standards.
- Provide students "The Old School Church Music Curricula."[6] This training includes specialized courses in choral techniques, graded choirs, student music methods, instrumental methods, and church music literature.

Pastors and church leaders have long made three assumptions regarding education for local church musicians. They assume our academic institutions:
- will graduate students with a practical understanding of local church needs,
- will capture a sense of mission with their congregations, and
- will equip and train worship leaders to meet the demands of congregations immersed in twenty-first-century culture.

The question is, Are we actually doing this?

Over the past decade in response to these expectations, college presidents and administrators pushed church music departments to establish worship degree programs with less emphasis on music and more focus on Christian disciplines. In response, many music educators raised the flag of accreditation requirements and resisted change. The accreditation obstacle, however, has forced the National Association of Schools of Music (NASM) to begin development of standards for worship training.

A CHANGE IN STANDARDS

Founded in 1924, NASM is comprised of nearly 650 member institutions that establish national standards for undergraduate and graduate degrees and other credentials. Until recently, their standards for church music degrees closely paralleled those for most secular music degrees. Acknowledging the changing paradigm, in 2013 NASM instituted new "standards for worship studies degrees" for inclusion in the NASM handbook. Member schools now have the option of offering "interdisciplinary bachelor of music degrees" in worship studies, worship and music, worship leadership, worship ministry, worship arts, etc.

While the changes in NASM standards are encouraging and open the door for additional adjustments, an important reality remains: the old-school curriculum in church music equipped our students for the wrong market. Some argue this happened because the model was faulty from the beginning.

The evangelical community has always been driven by the popular music of the day. During the 1940s and 1950s when the old-school model was developed, Southern Baptist and other mainline churches were following the seminary model by developing a classical education approach. By contrast, Pentecostal groups, radio-driven ministries (later TV ministries), and personality-focused churches were already using popular music genres as the main source for leading and developing personnel for worship. Though some will disagree, the fact remains that by the mid-1960s structural cracks began to appear in the classical model due to a lack of relevance to the local church market. Could it be the fault line was inadvertently built in when popular music genres were excluded from curricula design in the 1950s?

Regardless of when the problems developed, by the new millennium cries for a change of approach began to resonate. In 2005, only 7 schools offered undergraduate education in worship. As of 2013, more than 120 colleges and universities boast degrees (accredited and unaccredited) in worship studies, worship leadership, worship and music, worship technology, worship ministry, worship arts, and more.[7] A simple review of the degree requirements, however, shows there is no norm upon which to build a unified curriculum. A national standard must be established specifically for worship education, not simply a modification of sacred music or church music degrees.

There also must be balance in our teaching. Some skills are nonnegotiable, regardless of the stylistic approach or identity of a church. The question is not should students be trained in music theory, but rather what type of theory will be taught: traditional or commercial. Should the modern worship leader be able to analyze a Bach chorale or lay out a chart based on Nashville Numbers? Students will need quality instruction in vocal techniques and performance, but should a classical repertoire or songs relating to the modern worship movement be the driver? Will conducting education be directed at large choirs or small vocal teams? Will instrumental arranging focus on orchestras or worship bands? While the answers are probably a mixture of all the above, these issues must be addressed as standards are expanded over the ensuing years.

CULTURAL DEMANDS

In a 2011 survey of National Association of Schools of Music member schools, only 678 students were enrolled in church music-related degrees at 78 institutions. On average, 8.6 students were studying church music at NASM accredited institutions. In 2012, only 70 undergraduate, 78 graduate, and 8 doctoral students received degrees at NASM member schools.[8] Why are those numbers so low?

According to research at Liberty University, between 2,800 and 3,000 job openings exist for worship leaders, pastors, and support staff in the evangelical community alone.[9] Why are so many churches not turning to our colleges and seminaries to find trained and equipped personnel? Consider these statistics:

- Sixty-one percent (187 million) of the American population are under the age of 45.
- Twenty-six percent (81 million) are between the ages of 45 and 64.
- Thirteen percent (40 million) are over the age of 65.

Do pastors and church leaders perceive the vast majority of colleges and universities offering degrees in church music have built their curriculum around the needs of a demographic that is over the age of 65? If 61 percent of the American population are under the age of 45, how do we expect to appeal to their spiritual, emotional, and artistic needs if our programs primarily accommodate the senior adult? Even if classrooms were filled, are we teaching the right kind of curricula to prepare students to work in twenty-first-century evangelical churches?

The challenge of teaching worship leading skills to millennials is much deeper and more complicated than simply developing musical and technological savvy. Core philosophies and preferences must be revisited and methodologies must be overhauled, which often meet resistance from the academic community. In dealing with this reality someone has asked, "Should we as educators continue to 'guard the casket of tradition' just so we can hold fast to the constructs that originally led us to create church music degrees?"

A MODEL FOR CURRICULA DEVELOPMENT

The curricula for worship degrees at Liberty University are built on five foundational principles addressing character building, integrity, spiritual discernment, and a spirit of servant leadership. These serve as a model, or set of constructs, used to guide the curricula-building process. Vernon M. Whaley, dean of the School of Music at Liberty University, identifies these principles as:

Formational—Curricula must be designed to assist in shaping and forming young lives.

Transformational—Curricula must be structured so student lives are transformed and changed through participation in skills courses, applied studies, and various internship and practicum opportunities.

Relational—Curricula must focus first on our upward relationship with God and include serious discipleship, instruction in the Christian disciplines, and how to practice lifestyle worship. Curricula must also address horizontal relationships with fellow students and with faculty as mentors, counselors, or advisors. It should also include opportunities for student interaction, group projects, worship teams, and small-group Bible study.

Missional—Built into our curricula should be the opportunity to serve, share, evangelize, and proclaim the gospel of Jesus Christ.

Reproducible—Embedded in the curricula should be opportunities for the student to teach, train, and equip others as worshippers.[10]

CHRISTIAN IVORY TOWERS

Those who are in the academic world have been accused of being out of touch with reality, popularly referred to as being in an "ivory tower." While there are always exceptions, this accusation is true for many institutions that train worship leaders. While some professors served churches early in their ministries, or continue to serve on a part-time basis on weekends, most do not have a history of successful ministry in the local church.

Medical schools have a much better model. Students training to be vascular surgeons are trained by professors who perform the procedure on a regular basis. How many would sign up for heart surgery with a physician who had not successfully performed the procedure in years? While worship education involves teaching foundational elements in philosophy and theology, the curriculum must also be practical in order to be effective. The key is a finding a healthy balance.

While this tension between market demands and academic ideals became more visible after 1990, it has always been there. In his book, *Jubilate II: Church Music in Worship and Renewal*, Don Hustad, longtime professor of church music at Southern Baptist Theological Seminary, calls himself a "schizophrenic musician," referring to the disconnect between his classical music experiences in the academic world, as opposed to the reality faced in church settings. As the contemporary worship movement systematically displaced classical church music in the local church, the schizophrenia compounded.

As accrediting standards are reviewed and curricula expanded over the next decade, educational institutions must include local church practitioners in the teaching faculty. In fact, would it be outrageous to require those teaching courses such as The Role of Worship Leader and Building Relationships in Worship to have local ministry credentials? New models for faculty involvement must be developed to include an increased usage of adjunct and guest faculty with successful worship ministry experience.

Students deserve to be taught by competent faculty experienced in the worship ministry in the local church. Educational institutions must develop strategies to make this a reality.

SO WHAT SHOULD IT LOOK LIKE?

First, worship curricula should provide a platform where students can nurture and thoroughly understand their calling. Students must understand the biblical basis for their calling and the opportunities, responsibilities, and parameters of being obedient to God's call upon their lives.

Second, any curricula must equip worship leaders as skilled music professionals. This includes a thorough dose of worship theology, principles of leadership, Old and New Testament principles for worship, history and philosophy of worship, a clear understanding of creative worship, and a variety of opportunities to apply the learned principles to ministry. They need to be skilled singers, players of instruments (the more the better), conductors, communicators of the gospel, and confident in their ability to work with people.

Third, the curricula should meet the expectations of any accredited baccalaureate degree, complete with studies in the liberal arts, sciences, and languages.

Fourth, young professionals should receive ongoing training from practitioners already in the field. Ideally, this should include resident and guest teachers that have years of life experience working as worship leaders and ministers of music. The heart of short- and long-term mentoring should center on a strong emphasis on in-the-field experiences, such as practicums and internships opportunities.

Fifth, the curricula should be market-driven. It should equip students for specific tasks in the evangelical job market. Students must be prepared to meet the challenge of successfully fulfilling the various roles required of a full-time worship pastor. Students also need equipping in worship programming, musical performance, drama, Scripture reading, and songwriting.

Sixth, any curriculum should equip students to handle a broad range of worship-related technologies. Students must have basic competencies in sound, lighting, and video-related skills.

Seventh, programs must be designed that provide strong business skills in leadership, finance, planning processes, and administration. Organizational and interpersonal communication skills also are critical to the success of the modern worship leader and should be foundational in any curricula design.

Eighth, any program dedicated to the training of worship leaders must connect with the local church. After all, this is a program of study to train musicians for local church ministries. As such, the skills taught should reflect actual market need and be experienced based.[11]

CONCLUSION

For more than 70 years, seminaries and evangelical colleges have trained musicians for service in the local church. Though well intended, after 1990 most degree programs ceased to reflect the actual skills required for successful ministry. Church musicians willing to expand their traditional skill sets were able to successfully navigate the changing worship culture. Those who could not, or would not, did not survive.

Although the number of worship-related positions is increasing, the number of students involved in church music-related academic programs is declining. This infers the worship positions are being filled with worship leaders who have little formal musical and theological training, thus creating additional challenges that will be discussed in another chapter.

In order to stop the bleeding and equip the next generation of worship leaders, seminaries and colleges must drastically overhaul their training approach. Additionally, accrediting agencies, such as NASM, must reevaluate the standards by which these programs are judged. While skills in areas such as voice, piano, conducting, and theory are needed, these must be balanced and infused with training in commercial theory, technology, pop instruments, business competencies, and worship theology. It is not 1970. The worship culture is dramatically different. Let us diligently train worship leaders to serve the churches of this generation, not those churches that ceased to exist more than two decades ago.

CHAPTER 5

Worship Under a Flag of Truce:

NAVIGATING A POSTWORSHIP WAR CULTURE

The date: December 17, 1944. The location: the remote Philippine island of Lubgang. In those waning days of World War II, 23-year-old Hiroo Onoda, a lieutenant in the Imperial Japanese Army, was deployed to this tiny island to lead a small band of soldiers in guerrilla warfare against Allied troops. Onoda's orders were clear and pointed:

> You are absolutely forbidden to die by your own hand. It may take three years, it may take five, but whatever happens, we'll come back for you. Until then, so long as you have one soldier, you are to continue to lead him. You may have to live on coconuts. If that's the case, live on coconuts! Under no circumstances are you [to] give up your life voluntarily.

The war ended nine months later, but no one told Onoda.

Over the ensuing years, Onoda and his three fellow soldiers continued fighting while taking cover in the jungle. Leaflets dropped from airplanes in an attempt to communicate the war's outcome, but Onoda and his men viewed this as propaganda. Numerous search parties attempted to locate Onoda and his fellow soldiers to stop their fighting. Again, following orders, Onoda's party fired on many of these parties thinking they were enemy patrols. As ordered, Onoda and his men continued to fight and refused to surrender.

Over the years the group declined: one member actually surrendered and two others died. Onoda was the lone survivor, continuing to fight, hide, and evade. On March 9, 1974, Onoda's commanding officer, who had long since moved on from the war, returned to the island and convinced Onoda the war was over and Japan surrendered. Onoda handed over his weapon and walked out of the jungle . . . 29 years after the war ended.

Many in our churches resemble Hiroo Onoda: they continue to fight a war that is over. Moving on from full-fledged combat, most churches entered what Mark Galli, editor of *Christianity Today,* calls a "tense truce." Some, however, continue to mount a guerilla warfare, firing sniper shots over musical style preference. Even so, all signs indicate the majority of church members acknowledge the changes that emerged during the worship renewal of the past 30 years. Everyone is not happy, but the weapons largely have been put away.

Thom S. Rainer highlighted the importance of musical style preference in "3 Signs Worship Wars May Be Ending," an article he contributed to *The Christian Post* (christianpost.com):

> For decades church members have been fighting, splitting, and lamenting the state of music in our worship services. But when all is said and done, it's largely about preferences. And no issue seems to bring out the worst in us like our preferred music style.
>
> Many worship leaders should get hazard pay.
>
> While I'm not crazy enough to predict the total cessation of worship wars, I am willing to say that they will be ending in many churches.

Several factors are contributing to a positive shift in the climate of modern worship culture. First, a growing number of churches through intentional efforts are reuniting a family that far too long stood divided over musical style preferences. After decades of fighting over the types of songs to sing and instruments to use, we see a glimmer of hope that churches are finding common ground. While many churches still offer multiple services defined by style, others see value in a unified worship approach. These churches that once contributed to an us-against-them mentality by offering multiples services are changing.

Second, we are seeing more songs with stronger theology. In the early days of the contemporary worship movement, many people criticized the songs used in worship for their theological weakness. Adding insult to injury, the songs raised hostility with every repetition of each short phrase. How many worship leaders have endured the not-so-subtle jabs of church members referring to the day's worship set as "little ditties" or "7-11 songs . . . seven words sung 11 times"? By the way, has anyone ever counted the number of times *hallelujah* is used in Handel's "Hallelujah Chorus"?

These complaints, while often merited, are diminishing. As Rainer refers to as a "resurgence of hymnody," songwriters such as Keith and Krystin Getty, Chris Tomlin, and Michael Neale are making significant contributions to the modern hymn movement with songs such as "The Power of the Cross," "Jesus Messiah," and "Mercy Tree." These songs are replete with theological content and feature memorable melodies easily sung by congregations. Songwriters are now producing creative and inspiring arrangements of old hymns that help bridge the generation gap. Classic hymns such as, "All Hail the Power of Jesus' Name" and "Amazing Grace" are being reframed to speak to a new generation of worshippers. The modern hymn genre represents common ground for churches and will play a central role as we pursue a unified worship approach during the next decade.

Third, boomers and millennials genuinely seem to like each other and are willing to worship in the same room, facts pointed out by Rainer:

> The Christians of these generations desire to worship together. It's already fascinating to see worship styles meld as Boomers and Millennials come together. Admittedly, it's still a strong contemporary style, but the Boomers introduced secular culture to rock. Boomer Christians were among the first to embrace a more contemporary style of Christian music.

Fourth, many are simply tired of fighting. With more than 70 percent of Southern Baptist churches declining, church leaders realize as we fought inconsequential internal battles, our culture branded us as irrelevant. Staff and lay leadership of all ages are now standing up to stop the nonsense and refocus our singular true mission—reaching people for Christ. As mentioned in an earlier discussion, many church leaders are now focusing on that which Jesus focused on in his conversation with the woman at the well in John 4—that worship needs to be both spiritual and honest. Style is not as important as authenticity, content, and a genuine spirit of worship.

THE TRUCE IS FRAGILE

With the war largely over, skirmishes will continue within individual congregations strictly because the worship wars were fought over personal preference. If church leaders mishandle this transitional period, full hand-to-hand combat can quickly resume. This challenge of navigating our postworship war culture increases the difficulty of the transition.

Also, history is cyclical. As the millennials age, they too may resist efforts to change their preferred worship style, just as their parents and grandparents did. The millennials were raised expecting churches to acquiesce to their personal preferences. They will not surrender those preferences without some push back. It is possible (some will argue probable) the millennials will resist new approaches with a zeal that parallels, or even surpasses, the opposition offered by the boomers 30 years earlier. Stephen Miller highlighted this in an article for *Relevant* magazine (relevantmagazine.com) called, "The Modern Worship Wars":

> Ours is a generation marked by war.
> I'm not referring to a war with guns and tanks, though we have certainly seen our share of that as well. We are a generation that grew up witnessing the church fight over the very thing that was supposed to unite us: the worship of Jesus. . . .

Few of us emerged from these consumerism driven worship wars of our younger years unscathed. Their impact has been profound, both personally and corporately.

Fast-forward a decade or two and, at first glance, the worship wars that once plagued the church seem to have died down. So it might be easy to chalk it all up to a problem from a bygone era.

Until we walk out of a church service that didn't meet our own standards.

We have become professional critics of corporate worship. We complain about everything.

The volume is either too loud, or not loud enough. The lighting is either too bright or not bright enough; too showy or too bland.

We grumble about song selection, saying things like, "They introduce too many new songs," "Why do we keep doing the same songs over and over," or "I hate that song."

From key signatures to instrumentation; from the worship leader's fashion sense to vocal tone—it's all fair game for our consumer-driven critique.

A BIBLICAL RESPONSE

The idea of Christians operating under a truce is disgraceful. In fact, this idea is contrary to everything Scripture teaches about humility, forgiveness, and unity. The word *truce*, by definition, indicates unresolved issues remain and distrust exists. A truce infers personal preference still drives our decisions. These attitudes prevent the church from focusing on God as the object of worship and continue to place the focus on methodologies and styles.

HUMILITY

Pride drove the worship wars. People of all ages and musical style preferences shifted to a "What do I like?" approach that fractured many congregations. It was all about us. What happened to humility? Pride, the direct opposite of humility, manifests itself through attitudes of self-importance, egoism, and arrogance. Unfortunately, these characteristics defined many congregations over the past 30 years.

The Apostle Peter reminded all ages of humility's importance when he said:

> *Therefore, as a fellow elder and witness to the sufferings of the Messiah and also a participant in the glory about to be revealed, I exhort the elders among you: Shepherd God's flock among you, not overseeing out of compulsion but freely, according to God's will; not for the money but eagerly; not lording it over those entrusted to you, but being examples to the flock. And when the chief Shepherd appears, you will receive the unfading crown of glory.*
>
> *In the same way, you younger men, be subject to the elders. And all of you clothe yourselves with humility toward one another, because God resists the proud but gives grace to the humble. Humble yourselves, therefore, under the mighty hand of God, so that He may exalt you at the proper time, casting all your care on Him, because He cares about you.*
>
> (1 Peter 5:1–7)

C. S. Lewis wrote, "True humility is not thinking less of yourself; it is thinking of yourself less." Unfortunately, humility was a glaring omission in the worship wars.

FORGIVENESS

The battles of the past 30 years left plenty of blame to go around. Church leaders made many mistakes in our failures to cast vision, manage change, and disciple people through shifts in the worship culture. Through our failures, we spiritually injured countless people as worship services transitioned into trauma centers. Forgiveness must occur before we can move forward.

If anyone has caused pain, he has caused pain not so much to me but to some degree—not to exaggerate—to all of you. The punishment inflicted by the majority is sufficient for that person. As a result, you should instead forgive and comfort him. Otherwise, this one may be overwhelmed by excessive grief. Therefore I urge you to reaffirm your love to him.

(2 Corinthians 2:5–8)

UNITY

Christians must protect the Bride of Christ at all costs! We must never be agents of dissension and work to build unity with those we are called to serve. Unity is an important theme throughout Scripture and is central in our roles as worship leaders.

Psalm 133:1—"How good and pleasant it is when brothers live together in harmony!"

John 17:23—"I am in them and You are in Me. May they be made completely one, so the world may know You have sent Me and have loved them as You have loved Me."

Colossians 3:14—"Above all, put on love—the perfect bond of unity."

1 Corinthians 1:10—"Now I urge you, brothers, in the name of our Lord Jesus Christ, that all of you agree in what you say, that there be no divisions among you, and that you be united with the same understanding and the same conviction."

Philippians 2:1–4—"If then there is any encouragement in Christ, if any consolation of love, if any fellowship with the Spirit, if any affection and mercy, fulfill my joy by thinking the same way, having the same love, sharing the same feelings, focusing on one goal. Do nothing out of rivalry or conceit, but in humility consider others as more important than yourselves. Everyone should look out not only for his own interests, but also for the interests of others."

𝄢 WHAT NOW?

World War I, with its trench warfare and hand-to-hand combat, was one of the bloodiest conflicts in world history. As Christmas 1914 approached, the German army fiercely battled the British and French forces on the battlefields of Flanders. Both sides dug in, safe in muddy, man-made trenches six to eight feet deep that seemed to stretch on for days.

Christmas trees began to appear outside German trenches. Songs filled the air and a hope of peace spread across the battlefield. The British and French troops responded with their own Christmas celebrations, singing songs in their native language.

No one knows how it started, but the soldiers somehow negotiated a spontaneous truce, referred to by many historians as the Christmas miracle of 1914. Soldiers who hours earlier engaged in fierce battle, met in "no-man's-land," that space between opposing armies, to shake hands, bury dead men, and exchange gifts such as postcards, newspapers, and stories of family.

The truce, though inspiring, ended. The same soldiers who shared a fleeting moment of peace climbed back into their trenches and resumed the battle. We must prevent the resumption of battle in our churches! How do we prevent the worship wars from reigniting?

BE STRATEGIC IN DEVELOPING RELATIONSHIPS

Our ministries are defined by relationships. John Maxwell correctly said, "People don't care how much you know until they know how much you care." This statement underscores an important point: Our ability to lead others to worship will largely depend on the strength of our relationships . . . especially in a postworship war culture accented by uncertainty and a lack of trust. When the last notes of our ministries fade away, people will not remember if we were great singers or conductors, but were we there for them in their darkest moments.

Very few worship leaders lose their jobs over a lack of musical abilities. Churches usually assess these before employing a person for the position. By contrast, churches dismiss countless worship leaders every week because of their inability to get along with people. We are not in the music business; we are in the people business. Those who ignore this truth do so at their own peril.

We (the authors) both deal regularly with worship leaders as well as other ministers who simply do not understand the need to develop, enhance, and maintain personal relationships within their ministries. The result is broken and severed relationships across the land.

Romans 12:9–21 outlines a specific set of character traits that, while applicable to all Christians, are especially relevant to church leaders in this postworship war culture. In some ways, this passage serves as a personality profile for successful worship leaders and helps define the attributes required to build strong relationships with those we are called to serve.

C PERSONALITY PROFILE OF POSTWORSHIP WAR LEADERS—ROMANS 12:9–21

Genuine (v. 9)—"Love must be without hypocrisy. Detest evil; cling to what is good."

Have you ever know someone who lacked authenticity? People follow leaders they trust. For this to occur, our public image must match the life we live in private. How we deal with our teams must be consistent. Are your actions genuine?

- Do you run down members of your team?
- Are you guilty of gossiping about people in your ministry?
- Is your "platform image" inconsistent with your lifestyle?
- Are your actions marked by integrity?

Caring (v. 10)—"Show family affection to one another with brotherly love. Outdo one another in showing honor."

We all innately desire to be loved and appreciated. Demonstrating a caring attitude to members of our church families and our ministry teams goes a long way in building lasting relationships that positively impact ministry. For example, visiting hospitals and nursing homes encourages the patients as well as the person making the visit. Some people have a natural gift for this type of ministry, while others have to be intentional. Either way, pastoral care must be a priority in our ministries.

Similarly, we need to contact those in our ministries on their birthdays and wedding anniversaries. For example, Frank called every church member on his or her birthday until he was in a church with more than 1,000 members! Technology allows us to easily set reminders of special days into our calendars or phones. A simple text message or phone call tells people you are thinking about them. Recognizing important milestones, such as job promotions or civic awards, is always well received. Also, attending special events (i.e., graduations, weddings, and concerts) shows people we value them and honor the accomplishments in their lives. The possibilities are endless. We simply must make the effort to find practical ways to demonstrate a caring attitude to those we serve.

Enthusiastic (v. 11)—"Do not lack diligence; be fervent in spirit; serve the Lord."

Building quality relationships takes persistent effort. It requires an enthusiasm and a desire to know individuals on a personal level.

1. Ministry directory—A useful tool is a ministry directory compiled for your personal use. Have the members of your ministry complete a short biographical sketch and take a photo. Place this information in a notebook, or upload it to your computer or phone for quick reference. Then, when you pass someone in the hallway, you can call them by name or ask about their families. These simple things add credibility to those charged with leading ministries.

2. Home visits—One of the most impactful actions in relationship building is development of an intentional strategy for visiting in the homes of those you serve. When moving to a new ministry location, try to make a home visit to every worship team member in the first year! While this may sound overwhelming, it builds a sense of unity and family that is hard to replicate. The visits should be brief, usually 30 minutes, and focus on their family, how they met their spouse, where they work, etc. With that effort, you are now viewed as their friend, not simply a hired church staff member.

3. Phone calls—Make it a priority to telephone each team member regularly. Our technology-driven culture overwhelms people with emails, blog posts, and text messages. Because of this, a periodic personal contact is always well received. First Baptist Jackson has more than 325 members in the sanctuary choir, and the phone calls take two full days to complete. Though a substantial investment of time, it is worth the effort to connect with individual worship ministry members one-on-one. An added benefit is that these personal contacts usually increase rehearsal attendance by 20 percent during the following weeks.

4. Be fun to be around! This verse talks about being "fervent in spirit." In other words, show a passionate enthusiasm for what we do. Learn to laugh and engage with people in a manner that makes them want to be around you.

Positive, Patient, and Prayerful (v. 12)—"Rejoice in hope; be patient in affliction; be persistent in prayer."

Do you ever *honestly* look into the eyes of those seated in your worship services? If you do, here is what you see:

- a family on the brink of financial disaster
- a 40-year-old mom recently diagnosed with terminal cancer
- a college student struggling with alcohol abuse
- a high school girl dealing with guilt because of a recent abortion
- a husband and wife at the point of giving up on their marriage
- a young woman struggling with a decision to end her life
- a marriage imploding over infidelity and a lack of trust
- a teenage boy struggling with pornography addiction
- a child hiding the abuse that takes place in his or her home at night

Though many dress nicely and smile as though nothing is wrong, their lives are falling apart. These are the people we are called to lead each week. They need, more than anything, to know their leaders are praying for them and that Jesus Christ is the hope for all they face. As worship leaders we must never underestimate the power of encouragement! Make a commitment to pray for your team and for those in your congregation, and then find ways to connect with them on a spiritual level.

Hospitable (v. 13)—"Share with the saints in their needs; pursue hospitality."

This verse reminds us of the importance of being hospitable, thus treating people with kindness and affection.

1. Have people in your home. When we invite people into our homes, our relationships move to an entirely different level. While lunch meetings and group fellowship times are important, allowing people access to our personal space allows our friendships to go deeper.

2. Take advantage of the power of breakfast. Early morning meetings are a great time to conduct business and strengthen ministry relationships. Generally, early in the day our minds are clear of our routines that daily manage to bring frustrations, distractions, and challenges. Also, early morning meetings clear our night schedules so we can focus on our family commitments and retain balance in our lives.

3. Pick up the tab. Nothing builds friendship more than paying the bill! While not always possible, make every attempt to cover the meal, especially when you initiated the invitation.

Forgiving (v. 14)—"Bless those who persecute you; bless and do not curse."

It is difficult to forgive those who wrong us. Even so, we must be willing to apologize for the circumstance and attempt to find common ground for moving forward regardless of who was wronged (or perceived to be wronged). This is especially true for ministry relationships. Our attitude improves when we view those in our ministries as gifts, including those who—intentionally or not—harm us. While not easy to get there, arrival at this realization revolutionizes our ministry.

Church leaders often are the worst offenders, carrying grudges from conflicts occurring many years ago. Their anger focuses on:

- the deacon who voted against their recommendation,
- the senior adult who criticized their song choices,
- the choir member who complained about how they conducted rehearsals, or
- the pastor who provided corrective comments regarding some aspect of their ministry.

Unforgiving spirits and grudges are barriers to worship. We must intentionally address broken relationships and pursue a sense of reconciliation within our church families, especially in light of the damage resulting from years of internal fighting over music style. How can we lead those in front of us with broken relationships filling the room?

Experts in interpersonal relationships often point to the fact that many of the stated reasons of conflict are smoke screen issues. Often people bring into church settings, and particularly worship and worship style discussions, other emotional baggage, which manifests itself in extreme anger and overcompensation by emotionally acting out. It is imperative for worship leaders to discern the real reason for bursts of anger and internal fighting.

Sympathetic (v. 15)—"Rejoice with those who rejoice; weep with those who weep."

Our team members need us when an immediate family member dies. These ministry touches of support and encouragement build lasting relational ties that are not easily broken. In fact, when we make the effort to attend funerals for someone's spouse, parent, or child, we make a friend for life who will support our ministry when others fall away.

Unified (v. 16)—"Be in agreement with one another."

Worship leaders must be agents of unity. When we assume roles as Christian leaders, we give up our right to be critical of our senior pastor or fellow staff members. We forego the option of criticizing our church and its ministries. Unfortunately, staff members promoting a spirit of disunity and divisiveness often drive church conflict. This is not biblical behavior and must not be part of who we are as worship leaders.

Humble (v. 16)—"Do not be proud; instead, associate with the humble. Do not be wise in your own estimation."

Have you ever taken a personal inventory of how people see you? Do you come across as conceited or self-focused? Many church leaders struggle in this area. In managing this period of truce, less focus on our own preferences and focusing on what is best for the church will pay huge dividends.

Nonvindictive (vv. 17–21)

As Christians we are not to get even with those who wrong us. Judgment is not our responsibility. These verses clearly remind us that vengeance and wrath are in God's domain, not ours.

> *Do not repay anyone evil for evil. Try to do what is honorable in everyone's eyes. If possible, on your part, live at peace with everyone. Friends, do not avenge yourselves; instead, leave room for His wrath. For it is written: Vengeance belongs to Me; I will repay, says the Lord. But if your enemy is hungry, feed him. If he is thirsty, give him something to drink. For in so doing you will be heaping fiery coals on his head. Do not be conquered by evil, but conquer evil with good.*

INSIST ON SOLID THEOLOGICAL CONTENT

Music is neither sacred nor secular. In fact, the notes on paper, nor the sounds we hear, carry spiritual significance on their own. Granted, music can conjure up deep emotions from listeners, such as calmness, nostalgia, reflection, celebration, etc., but the lyrical content determines the message. When some hear the melody of "It Is Well with My Soul" or "The Old Rugged Cross," it creates an emotional connection with words they sang as a child.

The same melodies heard by someone who grew up outside the church may carry an entirely different meaning or carry no meaning at all. Divorced from the text, the music carries no spiritual meaning.

This separation of the impact of the music versus the lyrics is why the lyrical content of our songs is so important. The music serves as the vehicle, but the words deliver the message. Congregations more readily accept songs with strong theological content, regardless of style. We must intentionally develop a worship repertoire based on solid theological truth to help churches unify around our worship practice.

REMEMBER THAT CONTEXT DETERMINES STYLE

We often hear the statement that music is the universal language. If this is true, then that language certainly has many dialects! What is accepted by one as "beautiful" is viewed by another as "noise." Our life experiences and backgrounds most often shape these perceptions. Everything depends on context.

We must frame our worship services within the context of the culture we hope to reach. In the early years of international missions, missionaries traveled to foreign countries often attempting to Christianize entire cultures using the missionaries' own cultural approaches. This included everything from the structure of the services to the way new converts were made to dress.

In contrast, the developing field of ethnodoxology focuses on understanding how different cultures worship God and influences impacting those approaches. It goes beyond worship as an event because it studies how worship shapes, or is shaped, by culture. Central to this field is the concept of a "heart language." Joan Huyser-Honig describes the idea in her article for Calvin Institute of Christian Worship, entitled "Ethnodoxology: Calling All Peoples to Worship in Their Heart Language" (worship.calvin.edu):

> A key ethnodoxology concept is that we all have a heart language, the mother tongue in which we first learned to

express love, joy, sorrow, and need. Heart language is rich in nuance, humor, gesture, and inflection. It's the words you naturally dream in, the genres and images you use to change minds.

You may be thinking, *That is great for international missions, but I thought we were talking about the local church?* We are! We must use this same approach to engage local cultures with the message of Christ. If your church is located in rural Mississippi, the music might be Southern gospel. If in New York, could it be "black gospel"? In a border town in Texas, Hispanic sounds may define our musical approach. In some settings, it could be all of the above. Everything depends on context.

When a missionary prepares to move to an international culture, he or she spends years learning the language. It would be ludicrous to drop into the jungles of Thailand and attempt to reach that culture using English. The attempt to deliver a message to local communities in a musical language they do not understand is no different. It's all about the heart language.

INTENTIONALLY BUILD CONSENSUS

One of the most rewarding and, at times, difficult aspects of leadership is building consensus among those who do not agree. Navigating a postworship war culture requires strong leadership with the ability to get people on the same page. There are several steps we need to follow for this to happen.

UNIFY AROUND VISION

People follow a strategic and clear vision that is God-inspired and well articulated. As leaders we must define the target so people know without question where we are going. When people buy into the vision, things like passion, commitment, and excellence will follow. Most important, a clearly articulated vision allows people to unify around a common purpose. Ministries often struggle because there is no unifying vision to drive the people toward a common goal. Proverbs 29:18 says, "Without revelation [vision] people run wild, but one who listens to instruction will be happy."

Also, while understanding heritage is important, focus on the past can stymie a church's growth and passion. Volumes have been written on the shift from the institutional loyalty that defined the builder generation. While younger demographic groups can appreciate and at times celebrate heritage, it is not their focus. Visionary leadership is required to move them forward.

INVOLVE OTHERS IN DEVELOPING STRATEGY

Teams working together to solve problems bring a sense of unity and shared purpose. Because each demographic group brings unique perspectives and insight to the table, leaders must find ways to use multigenerational input when developing ministry strategies. Once people understand and support the vision, involve a wide range of personalities and interests in the strategy development. Your entire church will benefit.

FOCUS ON SHARED MINISTRY

We are best when we work together! Planning multigenerational ministry projects and missions efforts allows members of our team to labor beside one another, and to experience the power of God's movement as a family unit. Leaders must intentionally design opportunities that join all ages in sharing the love of Christ with our communities. Events such as block parties, worship ministry missions projects, and community service ministry events can help unify our congregations in a transitional worship culture.

CONCLUSION

William Tecumseh Sherman, the Union general famous for his "march to the sea" during the closing months of the Civil War, is credited with the quote, "War is hell." Churches know this all too well. The worship wars originated from the pits of hell and left carnage scattered through churches that fought individual civil wars. These battles effectively divided the Bride of Christ, with church leaders pitted against the very ones they were called to serve and church families lining up in opposition to one another other based on issues of personal preference and musical style. The only winner was Satan.

Thankfully, the battles are slowly ending. Isolated skirmishes will likely continue, yet all signs indicate that churches are picking up the pieces and moving forward. Challenges, however, remain. We must move beyond a truce to a new era of peace and unity in Christ's church. Over the next decade, churches must develop intentional strategies to build consensus anchored by strong relationships, a theologically sound worship repertoire, and contextualization of our worship culture. The generational connection between the boomers and millennials, who appear willing to focus on the future not mistakes of the past, is our best hope. Getting them on the same page will require visionary leadership and missional focus based on the Great Commandment and the Great Commission.

After 30 years of fighting, the war drums are becoming silent in many places. Christians are laying down their weapons and breaking down walls of musical style preference that have long divided us. Many simply realized that enough is enough. May we as church leaders rise to the occasion and lead people in authentic worship of the King of kings and Lord of lords . . . something that never should have divided us in the first place.

CHAPTER 6

Back from the Dead:

THE REEMERGENCE OF THE CHOIR IN MODERN WORSHIP

Some people suffer from taphephobia, a deep fear of being buried alive. According to one account, it happened to Marjorie Elphinstone during the first decade of the seventeenth century in rural Scotland. Marjorie, married to a wealthy landowner named Walter Innes, was buried wearing a small fortune in jewelry. As the story goes, the night after the funeral a thief dug up Marjorie and attempted to remove her expensive rings from her fingers. To his dismay, and most certainly shock, Marjorie awoke with a groan, sending the thief running for his life. Then, she proceeded to do what any self-respecting lady would have done: she gathered up her jewelry and walked home. Still in mourning, family members inside the house heard a very familiar knock at the door. Her husband, Walter, even commented to those present that if he had not seen Marjorie "dead and buried," he would have sworn it was her knock. Imagine their surprise when, upon opening the door, they saw her. Marjorie lived another 15 years before actually dying in 1622.

For years worship leaders and church growth experts boldly proclaimed, "The choir is dead!" Many churches reacted to these proclamations by moving away from using choirs since they were associated with nonrelevant worship practices. Those moves were premature. Though many choirs are on life support, a growing number are integral and thriving tools within the modern worship culture. Ultimately, life or death will be determined by the roles these choirs embrace.

EARLY DEVELOPMENTS

David W. Music traces the beginnings of choral singing in the United States (US) in "The Singing School, the Oxford Movement, and the Church Choir," for *Choral Journal*. Though choirs date back to Old Testament times, Music writes that they have only factored prominently into worship in the United States for just more than 200 years. Though isolated examples of choirs in the sixteenth and seventeenth centuries influenced by Moravian, Anglican, and Lutheran immigrants are documented, none substantially influenced the formation of choirs in American churches. As Music points out, the sad state of congregational singing became the driving force behind the introduction of choirs. Highlighted by rhythmic inconsistencies and out of tune a cappella singing, one early minister referred to the poor congregational singing as "howling"!

In response, Puritan ministers established singing schools to teach people "to read music, sing in rhythm, and keep pitch as they sang metrical psalms." The training usually consisted of weekly lessons, held over several weeks, and was extremely successful, both as a social event and in improving the quality of singers. Their intent, however, did not include the introduction of choirs into churches. Music refers to another source, Ralph T. Daniel's *The Anthem in New England Before 1800* when he states:

> The Puritan ministers who founded the singing school movement had no desire to introduce choirs into their churches; in fact, they would have objected to any such thing. Their goal was simply to improve congregational singing. There were invariably some members of the congregation, however, who participated in a singing school and others who did not. The singers naturally gravitated toward one another in a meeting house, perhaps at first forming a sort of informal body that by sheer volume and force of will began dominating the singing. Eventually, they agitated for an end to lining out, for the leadership of the

singing to pass from precentor [presenter] to themselves and their director, for a specific location in the meeting house that would be set aside for them, and for a time in the service in which they could sing more complicated music unencumbered by the congregation.

Eventually, the purpose of these trained singers changed from improving congregational singing to performing special music. Through the years, choirs moved from balconies to the chancel where they performed a featured anthem during each service. The balcony-to-chancel move had other implications. Singers now were in full view of the congregation, so robes became common to provide a consistent visual presentation, and the choir processional resulted from a logistical concern—the choir needed a way to get to the front of the room. By the twentieth century, many churches had incorporated choirs into their worship approaches, but their roles had changed dramatically: the groups trained to enhance congregational singing now were focused primarily on performance.

MAJOR INFLUENCES

Three primary influences in the 1940s and 1950s directly impacted the development of choirs in the local church. First was the growth of gospel radio broadcasts sweeping across the country. Radio came of age during the 1940s, with Franklin D. Roosevelt's fireside chats and radio shows such as *The Green Hornet* and *The Lone Ranger*. Running parallel to these were gospel broadcasts including *The Hour of Decision* with Billy Graham and *Old-Fashioned Revival Hour* with Charles E. Fuller. Second, the growth of church music programs in Bible colleges and seminaries influenced an entire generation of churches as men trained as conductors assumed leadership positions in churches across the United States. Third, stadium crusade events led by evangelists such as Billy Graham, Oral Roberts, and Bob Jones featured crusade songbooks and large choirs to support their revival efforts. Today's megachurch choir is a direct descendent from these types of events.

By the 1960s, the worship practices of churches with choirs varied significantly, largely dependent on culture and musical style preference. While a choir in a downtown church with a highly educated congregation might sing classical literature from Mendelssohn or Brahms, choirs in rural churches might adapt songs from the Stamps Baxter tradition or songs of personal experience like those of Bill Gaither. During the latter part of the decade, the youth movement added yet another influence to the musical preferences of local congregations.

The level of musical talent in churches was as distinct as the song choices. While churches in more formal settings covered multiple voice parts and could adequately present works such as *Messiah*, choirs in rural settings often sang unison, occasionally with improvised harmonies, hymns, or songs from the latest Southern gospel album. The common denominator in these approaches was the focus on performance.

During the 1980s, the evolution of choral literature to reflect influences from the worship renewal and the emergence of the CCM industry began. Songs recorded by CCM artists, such as Sandi Patty, became commonplace performances in churches across the land. Choral arrangers attempted to arrange popular Christian pop songs for choir, often with mixed results: the syncopated rhythms and melodic ranges often did not translate into singable choral arrangements. As a result, choral literature assumed a solo-driven approach, with choirs shifting to backing up the soloists, a style dominating the market since the early 1990s.

In the 1990s, churches within the contemporary worship movement began the shift from a choir-driven worship model to a model focused on praise teams. These teams used a small group, usually numbering from three to six singers assigned to soprano, alto, and tenor lines. The praise teams served these functional roles:

TEACHING NEW WORSHIP SONGS
Worship leaders needed an efficient way to teach new material to their

congregations. Smaller groups learned the songs quickly and provided solid reinforcement when the worship leader introduced the songs to the congregation. The smaller ensembles also more easily mastered the difficult rhythmic patterns and challenging ranges.

VOCAL REINFORCEMENT
Because worship teams used microphones, they provided strong vocal support for congregational singing.

HIGHER LEVEL OF MUSICAL TALENT
As the emphasis on higher quality increased with the rise of the CCM industry, even churches with limited resources could identify small groups of excellent musicians for worship teams though they might never find 30 to 50 good singers to fill a choir.

The use of praise teams became indelibly linked to the modern worship movement and continues in churches today. Though praise and worship teams assume various forms, the concept of using a small, highly skilled group of singers to reinforce congregational singing and lead worship is central to the modern worship movement.

A MOVE TO LIFE SUPPORT

The disparity between popular Christian music styles and choral-based literature caused many choirs to still embrace repertoire aimed primarily at an aging demographic. This was understandable to a degree: much of the choral literature originating from Christian publishing houses was rhythmically difficult, poorly written, or harmonically simplistic. Church choirs accustomed to singing challenging musical arrangements were faced with two options: (1) embrace the new choral approaches and face perpetual boredom, or (2) continue to use literature that no longer connected across local congregations. Most often the second option prevailed resulting in the "graying of the loft" as choirs became older, while many younger Christians chose to find other ways to praise God.

A NEW MODEL EMERGES

Though a growing number of churches shifted away from choirs, many church music leaders remained convinced of the choir's relevance to the modern worship culture. A new model emerged placing the primary emphasis on worship, not performance. Choirs still focused on musical concepts, but rehearsals now looked more like mini worship services, with Scripture and spiritual challenges interpolated throughout the experience. In most cases excellence and precision remained important, but a focus on worship—not the music—became the core value.

Rather than emphasizing anthems, choral responses, and calls to worship, the choir again became the primary support for congregational singing. While always a stated function of church choral groups, the shift to a performance-driven model beginning in the late nineteenth century obscured that purpose. Now choirs assumed the role of an expanded worship team. Though most worship choirs continued to present a special musical arrangement during each worship service, these selections were worship-driven and often featured praise teams and congregational participation.

Composers and arrangers fine-tuned many of their compositional approaches as this genre developed. While choral parts remained accessible for the untrained singer, orchestrators, such as Lari Goss and Camp Kirkland, redefined the genre with orchestrations that often elevated simplistic choral arrangements to new emotional and musical heights.

Technology became critical in redefining the role of choirs as worship leaders. Choral presentations often used video features designed to interpret the lyrical content of songs, a move designed to connect with a visually stimulated culture. Elements such as click tracks, drum loops, and musical stems, long a part of the commercial music industry, became common as churches attempted to mirror the sounds of the pop music culture. Many large choirs began prerecording core vocals, a practice that ensured a near flawless presentation as choirs joined the recording during worship. Responding to a consumer-driven church market emphasizing quality, smaller churches adopted similar models using split-track recordings to enhance the sound of their choirs. This often produces mixed results.

Since the early 2000s, the influence of popular media helped rebirth an interest in choral-based groups. Television talent shows such as *America's Got Talent*, *The Choir* (a BBC production), and *Clash of the Choirs* gave millennials and busters a positive experience with a medium they rendered irrelevant. Television series, such as *Glee*, along with hit movies, such as *High School Musical*, returned the "cool factor" to choral singing.

These cultural developments, coupled with excellent church models, have contributed to choirs reemerging as important players in the modern worship culture. Since the 1970s, new church starts and cutting-edge churches have made little to no use of choirs. This is changing as churches such as Church on the Move in Tulsa, Oklahoma, with a worship style closely paralleling pop music culture, reintroduce choirs in their worship times. While these groups looked nothing like the models of the 1980s and 1990s, they served the same function. Other megachurches, including Prestonwood Baptist Church, Irving, Texas; First Baptist Church, Woodstock, Georgia; Bellevue Baptist Church, Cordova, Tennessee; First Baptist Church, Dallas, Texas; and, First Baptist Church, Jackson, Mississippi, retain choir-driven worship approaches, using large choirs of 300-plus singers supplemented by praise teams and orchestra, to lead congregational worship.

Churches that left choirs for dead a few years earlier are once again embracing their importance. Granted, this new version looks, sounds, and functions differently, but it is a choir just the same. After decades on life support, the choir has reemerged as an important force in the modern worship movement.

𝄞 A BIBLICAL RESPONSE

The choir's biblical heritage dates back to at least the time of David. Since the early days of the Old Testament choirs have served a central function in the worship offered by God's people. During David's reign, musicians from the tribe of Levi were appointed to minister as part of tabernacle worship and later, after construction of Solomon's temple was complete, actually resided in the temple chambers where they ministered around the clock.

> *The singers, the heads of the Levite families, stayed in the temple chambers and were exempt from other tasks because they were on duty day and night. These were the heads of the Levite families, chiefs according to their gene-alogies, and lived in Jerusalem.*
>
> (1 Chronicles 9:33–35)

These Levitical musicians carried out musical responsibilities related to the worship of the Israelites and played a central role in the dedication of the Temple.

> *The Levitical singers dressed in fine linen and carrying cymbals, harps, and lyres were standing east of the altar, and with them were 120 priests blowing trumpets. The Levitical singers were descendants of Asaph, Heman, and Jeduthun and their sons and relatives. The trumpeters and singers joined together to praise and thank the Lord with one voice. They raised their voices, accompanied by trumpets, cymbals, and musical instruments, in praise to the Lord: For He is good; His faithful love endures forever. The temple, the Lord's temple, was filled with a cloud. And because of the cloud, the priests were not able to continue ministering, for the glory of the Lord filled God's temple.*
>
> (2 Chronicles 5:12–14)

Our churches need this same manifestation of the glory of God. This passage illustrates the role music and choirs can have in lifting up praise and adoration. When we do so with consecrated hearts, He will show His glory!

In 2 Chronicles 20, we see the importance of the choir as a lead warrior. Several of Israel's enemies joined forces to mount an attack against

God's people. In response, Jehoshaphat, king of Judah, called the nation to prayer, after which he sent forth a choir to lead into battle.

> *In the morning they got up early and went out to the wilderness of Tekoa. As they were about to go out, Jehoshaphat stood and said, "Hear me, Judah and you inhabitants of Jerusalem. Believe in Yahweh your God, and you will be established; believe in His prophets, and you will succeed." Then he consulted with the people and appointed some to sing for the LORD and some to praise the splendor of His holiness. When they went out in front of the armed forces, they kept singing: Give thanks to the LORD, for His faithful love endures forever. The moment they began their shouts and praises, the LORD set an ambush against the Ammonites, Moabites, and the inhabitants of Mount Seir who came to fight against Judah, and they were defeated. The Ammonites and Moabites turned against the inhabitants of Mount Seir and completely annihilated them. When they had finished with the inhabitants of Seir, they helped destroy each other.*
>
> (20:20–23)

Each week choirs lead our congregations into the throne room of God. Ephesians 6:12 reminds us that "our battle is not against flesh and blood, but against the rulers, against the authorities, against the world powers of this darkness, against the spiritual forces of evil in the heavens." While choirs of today do not fight physical wars, the battles are just as real and the conflicts just as significant. Worship is a place of spiritual battle and souls are the ultimate prize!

𝄢 WHAT NOW?

What does a modern worship choir look like? How do we transform our choirs into ones relevant to a modern worship culture? What should be their defining characteristics? All these important questions must be addressed as choirs are integrated into twenty-first-century worship approaches.

On the surface, modern church choirs may seem similar to those of previous generations. They are not! Churches attempting to simply maintain past choir models will see membership continue to decline, usually paralleling a downward trend in their overall church membership. Today's worship choir must be different by definition and in the way it functions.

WHAT DOES IT LOOK LIKE?

DEFINED BY PURPOSE

Reaching our culture for Christ requires a clearly defined purpose. Gone are the days when people attended church simply because it was the thing to do. Now our ministries must have a clearly defined purpose and add significance to the lives of those who participate. Sam S. Rainer III highlights this point in "Next Generation Needs," an article for *Christianity Today*:

> Older generations tended to place a higher priority on church activity and attendance. The younger generation, however, demands to know the purpose behind each activity. For Millennials, just attending church does not equal faithfulness. The only way they'll attend is if they see the church as being a meaningful part of their lives.

We must understand the choir cannot function on dated perceptions or approaches, but must be defined within the context of the targeted culture. Helping people embrace this vision requires visionary leadership and is a major challenge in redefining our approach to choir in the twenty-first century. This is where strong, visionary leadership is required. As leaders we must have the ability to see something that has yet to exist . . . and then help others see the same thing. Rainer explains:

Millennials don't reject the idea of authority, but they have redefined how authority is exercised. They tend to follow leaders who operate in a transformational capacity—and ones who aren't afraid to get their hands dirty. Rather than telling followers what the big picture is, these leaders allow followers to help create it. Transformational leaders inspire people to reach for a common goal, one developed through a shared vision.

In this environment, equipping and mentoring become more important than directing. Structure is looser, and what structure remains is not an end, but a means of helping people become disciples. Leading the members of the next generation requires a commitment to serve alongside them, not issuing directives from above them.

DRIVEN BY WORSHIP

One of the most striking traits of modern worship choirs is the freedom and passion they express. This differs greatly from the traditional choir approach that emphasized rigid formations, consistent posture, and all eyes on the director. While there is room for balance (singers still need to see interpretation, releases, cues, etc.), giving singers freedom as they worship is critical for choirs attempting to engage the culture. Just as contrasts in dynamics and tempo help communicate the lyrics of a song, body and facial language do the same. While not all worshippers are physically demonstrative, all should exhibit emotion from standing in the presence of God. Above all, worshippers must recognize a sense of freedom to show biblical expressions of worship.

In Luke 7 we find a beautiful example of a woman engaged in worship of our Lord. Her actions, though questioned by those around Jesus, were demonstrative and emotional as she responded to being in the presence of our Savior:

Then one of the Pharisees invited Him to eat with him. He entered the Pharisee's house and reclined at the table. And a woman in the town who was a sinner found out that Jesus was reclining at the table in the Pharisee's house. She brought an alabaster jar of fragrant oil and stood behind Him at His feet, weeping, and began to wash His feet with her tears. She wiped His feet with the hair of her head, kissing them and anointing them with the fragrant oil.

(vv. 36–38)

Passionate worship involves giving the best we have for a King who is worthy of it all! Modern worship choirs must communicate that passion, excellence, and precision.

CENTERED ON MINISTRY

A distinguishing characteristic of modern worship choirs is their desire for hands-on ministry experiences. People long to be part of something significant and meaningful. Singing on Sunday mornings was enough to draw people to our choirs 20 years ago. Now, that is no longer the case.

Choir leaders must develop strategies to use music as the tool that facilitates ministry opportunities. Concerts in nursing homes, hospitals, or detention centers allow choir members to directly encourage fellow Christians. Ministry, however, must transcend music. Workdays at orphanages, serving in soup kitchens or homeless shelters, and ministering to patients at the local cancer center are all ways choirs can have intentional ministry touches. Opportunities abound and are only limited by the lack of creativity or desire on the part of choir leadership.

Then the King will say to those on His right, "Come, you who are blessed by My Father, inherit the kingdom prepared for you from the foundation of the world. For I was hungry and you gave Me something to eat; I was thirsty and you gave Me something to drink; I was a stranger and you took Me in;

I was naked and you clothed Me; I was sick and you took care of Me; I was in prison and you visited Me." And the King will answer them, "I assure you: Whatever you did for one of the least of these brothers of Mine, you did for Me."

(Matthew 25:34–36, 40)

FOCUSED ON MISSIONS

The choir's ministry must be missional in nature. While this can involve short-term missions projects or trips, it is more about a change of core values. A missional focus must be at the heart of all we do, which then influences our approach to every aspect of our ministries. What was formerly a concert event becomes an opportunity to intentionally share Christ with those in attendance. This prompts questions such as the following:

- Why are we doing this presentation in the first place?
- Is this presentation based on mere tradition, or does it have a larger purpose?
- Are we planning a program to entertain or share Christ?
- What music will we select to effectively tell the story of redemption?
- How can we "change the audience" to reflect a larger number of unchurched attendees?
- Is the message of the gospel clear?

FILLING THE LOFT

Like worship services, healthy choirs must engage people of all ages. This presents a challenge for churches using age-segregated worship approaches. After all, how can you attract college students to choir when they attend another service? Exaggerating this challenge is the changing definition of commitment among younger generational groups. In the 1970s and 1980s, Builders with a strong level of commitment and deep institutional loyalty filled our choirs. Remember, this generation survived the Great Depression and united together to win World War II. Builders often worked for the same company their entire careers and attended the same church most of their lives. Choir members in this generation were present for rehearsals and worship services, with rare exceptions for sickness, work, or an occasional family vacation. In contrast, 60 percent of millennials change jobs every three years, and two-thirds never attend religious services. A 20-something choir member might attend rehearsal one night per month and yet consider himself or herself an active member.

Additionally, today's culture places added demands on families. The most limited commodity in our culture is discretionary time, and people seem to have less and less. The number of households with both parents working outside the home has steadily increased since 1969. Children's activities, such as youth sports, music lessons, and community service, often consume multiple nights each week, at times directly conflicting with previously protected "church times." Coupled with the desire of parents to manage homework and other responsibilities, these dynamics often leave young families harried and with limited time to give.

These challenges impact all aspects of our ministries, but especially the areas of scheduling, enlistment, and discipleship.

- Are rehearsal times and lengths once acceptable still working?
- Is the night we rehearse the best option?
- Will short-term commitments (four to six months) appeal more to potential choir members?
- What role does child care play in our programming?

We must ask these important questions because they determine how we approach and administer our ministries. Utilizing choirs in our worship services potentially involves a greater number of people in worship ministry—a strong benefit. While worship teams allow a select group of talented singers to serve in worship leadership roles, choirs allow average musicians a place of musical service in our churches. This being true, are there minimal requirements for choir membership?

While choir members need a basic singing ability, we must err on the side of ministry. A good sign is when people want to join your ministry with *no* musical talent! People are responding to the message, passion, and familial atmosphere. Even so, having an open-door policy does create challenges. At times potential choir members visit our rehearsals . . . and they cannot match pitch! How do you handle these well-intentioned folks?

While our choir membership is not auditioned, we do schedule a time to hear everyone sing. During this time, we ask about their relationship with the Lord, identify specific prayer requests, and ask them to sing a familiar hymn or worship song. While the general rule is we take everyone, these meetings help identify those who may need added vocal coaching or present special musical challenges. Remember, there will be many people in our ministries who need us more than we need them. Our first priority is ministry.

A young girl presented such as challenge in one of our churches. Gayle loved to sing, but limitations of Down syndrome left her with weak musical skills. What she lacked in skill, however, was made up in enthusiasm. Though she did not know a lot of modern worship songs, when we sang an old hymn like "Victory in Jesus" or "Amazing Grace," Gayle dictated the tempo with the sheer volume of her voice.

One Sunday morning, Gayle came into the choir room to robe up with the choir. We gently directed her back to the worship center by simply telling her, "Not this week, Gayle." Our response was performance-driven. How could Gayle sing with the choir? She would ruin the anthem. After several weeks, Gayle got the message. She quit trying.

A few weeks later, we heard Gayle had been hospitalized due to complications from diabetes. After arriving at her hospital room, her health rapidly deteriorated, and she died a short time later. This was a major shock because Gayle was deeply loved by our congregation.

Arriving home that evening, Lavon told his wife about Gayle's death. Her response was immediate and pointed. Never looking up from the sink as she washed dishes, she simply said, "I guess she's being allowed to sing in the choir today." It was a blow to the gut. Had we deprived this sweet girl of the opportunity to "make a joyful noise the Lord" (Psalm 100:1 KJV)? Did our focus on quality outweigh the mandate of ministry? While the reality was

Gayle was not physically able to sing in the choir, the handling of her desire to worship and lead in worship was completely wrong.

From that point forward, our choir paradigm shifted: our choir is open to everyone. The person with the music degree, the functional singer, and, yes, the monotone! Does this present challenges? Absolutely. We strategically seat people and move them away from microphones every week. Most times nonsingers realize that choir is not best suited for them and connect with other ministries. Where we can, we redirect them to other ministries. We never turn people away. At the end of the day, it is not about the music!

CONCLUSION

After several years of decline, many churches are now rediscovering the passion and energy choirs can bring to modern worship experiences. This modern version does not look or sound the same as in earlier generations, but by redefining its identity within the context of current culture, choirs have reemerged as an important part of worship.

Over the next decade, church choirs that refuse to adjust literature and methodologies will find themselves in rapid decline. Those that recalibrate to connect with culture, especially the millennials, will thrive. Others not willing to make these changes will cease to exist. Old stereotypes must be discarded and new identities defined. A passion for using music in worship, ministry, and missions must be the new standard replacing the performance standard that existed in the United States for almost 200 years.

After three decades of being on life support, a growing number of choirs are showing signs of new spiritual life. Whether they live or die is totally dependent on the choices they make. It is a matter of life and death.

CHAPTER 7

A Theological Melting Pot:

THE LOSS OF THEOLOGICAL DISTINCTIVENESS

> Theology is practical: especially now. In the old days, when there was less education and discussion, perhaps it was possible to get on with a very few simple ideas about God. But it is not so now. Everyone reads, everyone hears things discussed. Consequently, if you do not listen to Theology, that will not mean that you have no ideas about God. It will mean that you have a lot of wrong ones—bad, muddled, out-of-date ideas. For a great many of the ideas about God which are trotted out as novelties today are simply the ones which real Theologians tried centuries ago and rejected. To believe in the popular religion . . . is retrogression—like believing the earth is flat.
>
> —C. S. Lewis, *Mere Christianity*

In 1935, B. B. McKinney's immediate challenge upon becoming music editor for the Baptist Sunday School Board in Nashville was the state of theological confusion of congregational music across the Southern Baptist Convention. With no official denominational hymnal, churches used a hodgepodge of songbooks and hymnals representing all sorts of theological beliefs. The publication of *The Broadman Hymnal* in 1940 changed this dynamic. *The Broadman Hymnal* broke new ground, with its most significant role being the unification of Southern Baptist hymn repertoire. Southern Baptists, for 50 years, sang from a common pool of hymns providing a consistency in theology and congregational songs.

Robert D. Dale, in *To Dream Again: How to Help Your Church Come Alive*, asserts, "The hymns a congregation sings regularly and with feeling are the best clue to the congregation's corporate theology" and "the person who chooses the hymns for worship is potentially the most important theologian in his congregation." If these assertions are true, we are in trouble. Today the supply of theologically unvetted worship songs is vast. Continued use of these songs in worship through the next decade will lead to the continuing breakdown of the distinct theological characteristics that defined churches for decades in favor of a convergent theology integrating beliefs from across the theological spectrum. That a growing number of Christians indicate they are customizing their faith, not following any one theological belief system, confirms this integration of beliefs.[1]

HOW DID WE GET HERE?

One of the primary arguments against the contemporary worship movement was theologically weak songs. This same characteristic, ironically, may be one of the reasons for its success. By avoiding divisive doctrinal and theological positions, songs focused on God's majesty, the Cross, and salvation, easily connected with Christians from all evangelical traditions, which was not a bad thing. Christian culture is too often divided over trivial positions, so finding common ground around major theological beliefs brings unity and shared purpose. Danger emerges when key doctrinal beliefs gradually erode or theological views defining a group are lost. Unfortunately, our worship songs may be a primary driver in this loss of theological integrity.

The loss of theological distinctiveness increased over the past two decades as worship leaders ignored a need for formal theological education. The development of solid theological foundations became a self-guided experiment when seminary or Bible degrees were no longer required for the worship leaders in our churches. The modern worship leader, equipped with a Bible, guitar, and a good voice, often assembles his or her worship philosophy and theology from various sources including conferences, prominent worship leaders/artists or the "flavor of the day" parachurch movement. These influences can positively impact the development of a solid biblical and theological understanding of worship; however, if not cautious, these influences could lead to a hybrid perspective, mixing Pentecostalism with various theological traditions and worship practices. The result: theological confusion.

In their research of emerging trends, the Barna Group (barna.org) affirms:

> What used to be basic, universally-known truths about Christianity are now unknown mysteries to a large and growing share of Americans—especially young adults. . . . studies in 2010 showed that while most people regard Easter as a religious holiday, only a minority of adults associate Easter with the resurrection of Jesus Christ. Other examples include the finding that few adults believe that their faith is meant to be the focal point of their life or to be integrated into every aspect of their existence. Further, a growing majority believe the Holy Spirit is a symbol of God's presence or power, but not a living entity. As the two younger generations . . . ascend to numerical and positional supremacy in churches across the nation, the data suggest that biblical literacy is likely to decline significantly. *The theological free-for-all that is encroaching in Protestant churches nationwide suggests the coming decade will be a time of unparalleled theological diversity and inconsistency.*

> (author's emphasis)

Are the songs we select for worship contributing to this "theological diversity and inconsistency"? As an exercise, review your church's worship times for the past six months, focusing on the songs. Ask these questions:

- What theological truths are being taught to your church?
- Is the focus of these songs primarily God's greatness?
- What other attributes of God are addressed in these songs?
- Do the songs address sin, confession, or missions?
- Do the songs teach accurate theological views of the Trinity, atonement, and ministry?
- Do the songs make doctrinal statements that contradict our theological views as a church or denomination?
- If your congregation's view of God was based *exclusively* on the song selection, what would God look like?

A THEOLOGICAL BUFFET?

We are all shaped by influence from varying sources. Positive and negative influences work together to form our philosophies and theological foundations. We must understand these influences to critically and honestly assess what shapes our theology. Songs may be useful for worship, even if we do not agree on every point, but understanding key theological differences is necessary to prevent the introduction of heretical teaching to our churches.

Songs in worship representing many theological perspectives is nothing new. Hymnals of days gone by were filled with the writings of Methodists, Baptists, Congregationalists, Lutheran, Catholic . . . and everything in between. In fact, Ralph Vaughan Williams, music editor for *The English Hymnal*, was likely an atheist! Likewise, the appearance of bad theology in worship music is nothing new and will never be completely eliminated. Even so, church leaders can protect congregations from errant doctrine by subjecting new worship literature to proper theological vetting.

Today, the number of worship songs is astronomical. The sheer numbers of songs available raises several challenges. In the days of printed hymnals, theology/doctrine review committees examined the content of each hymn proposed for inclusion in the denominational hymnal. Comprised of pastors, educators, and local church musicians, this committee served as gatekeepers, ensuring the content passed through the hymnal was theologically sound. The mid-1990s shift to the large-screen projection of song lyrics, while bringing many positive changes to worship, marked the beginning of a steady decline in the demand for printed hymnals. Additionally, as the Internet became a way of life, songwriters quickly disseminated new songs to large numbers of people. The loss of hymnal usage combined with the almost overnight integration of songs into worship pushed the decline of theological review. Today we find ourselves back at the exact position that originally drove the publication of denominational hymnals such as *The Broadman Hymnal*: theological confusion resulting directly from congregational songs.

We are not arguing to turn back the clock and return to hymnals while avoiding all new worship songs. In fact, the opposite is true. Using new worship songs keeps the church connected to modern movements of God and brings a sense of creativity to worship. This positive connection injects a sense of relevance and passion into our churches. We are, however, pleading for theological integrity! To protect theological distinctions important to our identities, church leaders must be proactive in reviewing, evaluating, and testing the content of songs before the songs are introduced to congregations. The lack of theological training for worship leaders makes this difficult.

As the number of music and worship students pursuing seminary education declined, the new generation of worship leaders developed their theological positions as if they were buying lunch from an all-you-can-eat buffet: Pentecostalism for an appetizer, Reformed theology as an entrée, and a little Word of Faith for dessert. The resulting convoluted theology is comprised of any number of belief systems. That resulting theology then gets passed to our churches through the music selected for worship.

Someone once said, "To be forewarned is to be forearmed." The influences shaping the modern worship culture affirm this statement. While not necessarily negative, some influences are indeed problematic. All of them, along with the CCM industry, impact the theological content of songs within the modern worship movement and must be understood in light of their backgrounds, beliefs, and practices.

PASSION MOVEMENT

The Passion movement is synonymous with some of the most popular worship leaders of this generation, including Chris Tomlin, Kristian Stanfill, Christy Nockels, Matt Redman, and David Crowder. The songs birthed in this movement have incredible influence in the local church. Founded in 1997 by Louie Giglio and Jeff Lewis, the 2013 Passion Conference (268generation.com) drew more than 60,000 college students to Atlanta's Georgia Dome. The annual conference features pastors and teachers such as Francis Chan, Beth Moore, and John Piper and is responsible for sixstepsrecords (sixsteprecords.com) and the popular Passion worship CDs. The movement's music is highly influential, with many of the songs immediately integrated into the worship life of churches.

HILLSONG

Started by Brian and Bobbie Houston in 1983, Hillsong Church (located in Sydney, Australia) draws more than 30,000 worshippers to their multiple campuses each weekend. Founded as the Hills Christian Life Centre, a Pentecostal megachurch affiliated with the Australian branch of the Assemblies of God, the church changed its name to Hillsong Church in 1999 to capitalize on the success of the live worship recordings produced by the music ministry. Worship leaders Darlene Zschech, Reuben Morgan, and Joel Houston, among others, wrote many of the songs. Millions of copies of Hillsong's albums have been sold. With songs such as "Shout to the Lord," "The Power of Your Love," and "I Give You My Heart," Hillsong significantly influences the modern worship renewal across the world and continues to make contributions to the worship repertoire used in churches.

RESURGENCE OF REFORMED THEOLOGY

While not new, the debates surrounding Reformed theology are at heightened levels. While denominations, including Southern Baptists, are struggling to find common ground on this issue, an entire generation of Christian artists and songwriters has largely landed on the side of a "New Calvinism," influenced by leaders such as John Piper and Mark Driscoll. Conferences such as Desiring God (desiringgod.org/events) and Together for the Gospel (t4g.org) reinforce this New Calvinism and have revived interest in the writings of Jonathan Edwards and Charles Haddon (C. H.) Spurgeon. The movement's influence on contemporary Christian music was noted by *Time* magazine's David Van Biema:

> If you really want to follow the development of conservative Christianity, track its musical hits. In the early 1900s you might have heard "The Old Rugged Cross," a celebration of the atonement. By the 1980s you could have shared the Jesus-is-my-buddy intimacy of "Shine, Jesus, Shine." And today, more and more top songs feature a God who is very big, while we are . . . well, hark the David Crowder Band: "I am full of earth / You are heaven's worth / I am stained with dirt / Prone to depravity." Calvinism is back.

Based on the theology of John Calvin (1509–64), a system known as the five points of Calvinism was developed in the early seventeenth century and codified at the Synod of Dort in Holland in opposition to key teachings of Jacob Arminius and his followers. The five points often summarized by the acronym TULIP and nuanced by those who adhere to this view, include:

- Total depravity: People are spiritually dead and therefore unable to respond to God's offer of salvation unless He first regenerates them.
- Unconditional election: God chose some to be saved because He loved them, not because of any merit on their part.
- Limited atonement: Christ died only for the sins of the elect, not for everyone's sins.
- Irresistible grace: All whom God regenerates will inevitably choose to repent and exercise faith.
- Perseverance of the saints: God will preserve in salvation and eternal life those He saves.

While many Calvinists embrace only three or four points, many New Calvinist pastors and churches accept all five. Regardless of your stance on Reformed theology, with more than one-third of seminary graduates from Southern Baptist institutions describing themselves as Calvinists, this theological system will become more prevalent within the modern worship movement over the next decade.

In his role as president and CEO of the Executive Committee of the Southern Baptist Convention, Frank led the Southern Baptist Convention to encourage leaders from both Calvinist and non-Calvinist positions to work together more effectively. A document was signed by all of the members of that task force, which helped Baptists realize that we can work together in doing missions ministry and need to start talking to each other and not just at each other as had become the practice. While tensions will continue in this particular area, decisions and promises were made to pull together in a day and time where the world has one too many battles.

PENTECOSTALISM

A relatively modern phenomenon, tracing its origins to the Azusa Street Revival (1906) and boasting more than 500 million members worldwide, Pentecostalism is the largest and fastest-growing segment of Christianity. While Pentecostals hold to core doctrines of the Trinity, the deity of Jesus Christ, and the belief that the Bible is the Word of God, their unifying belief is in a "unique gifting of the Holy Spirit," specifically the "gift of tongues." Most Pentecostals believe baptism in the Holy Spirit and the gift of tongues is required for salvation. There are many different denominations within the Pentecostal movement, including the Assemblies of God, the Church of God in Christ, the Church of God, the International Church of the Foursquare Gospel, the United Pentecostal Church International, and the International Pentecostal Holiness Church.

Many popular Christian songwriters are from this tradition, including Phillips, Craig, and Dean (United Pentecostal International Church) as well as Reuben Morgan and Darlene Zschech (Assemblies of God). Through these songwriters, the influence of Pentecostalism is immense across the spectrum of modern worship, as pointed out by Larry Eskridge in "Slain by the Music," published in *The Christian Century* (christiancentury.org):

> Indeed, an argument could be made that at no time since the First Great Awakening have so many churches of disparate denominational, theological and stylistic approaches been so united in terms of their music: one can now walk into old-line Pentecostal churches, small-town evangelical congregations, mall-like suburban megachurches, and many a mainline Protestant sanctuary across the country on any given Sunday morning and hear the same hymns and choruses done in approximately the same musical styles, with similar settings and instrumentation.

TELEVISION

As the popularity of television spread following World War II, a generation of preachers took to the airwaves to expand their influence and teaching. Televangelists such as Oral Roberts and Rex Humbard, who in 1952 was the first to broadcast a weekly church service on television, reached large audiences by combining popular music, preaching, and charismatic personalities. Roberts introduced viewers to theological teachings of healing, prosperity gospel, and Pentecostalism, and built a financial and broadcast empire.

By the 1970s, Christian programming grew in popularity with broadcasts such as *The Old Time Gospel Hour* (Jerry Falwell), *Jimmy Swaggart Telecast*, and *The PTL Club* (Jim and Tammy Faye Bakker) filling the airwaves. Today there are more than 100 religious networks representing every extreme of theological and doctrinal positions, including Trinity Broadcasting Network (TBN), God TV, National Religious Broadcasters (NRB), Global Catholic Network (EWTN, or Eternal Word Television Network), and the Christian Broadcasting Network (CBN). These networks carry 24/7 programming featuring a wide range of theological perspectives. For example, TBN, the world's largest Christian television network, broadcasts sermons by Southern Baptist leaders such as Ed Young Sr., James Merritt, and the late

Adrian Rogers, oftentimes juxtaposed with Word of Faith teachers Creflo Dollar, Joyce Meyer, Jesse Duplantis, and Benny Hinn. With such a disparity of beliefs, the potential for theological confusion on the part of the viewer is obvious.

WORSHIP CONFERENCES

Conferences and training events designed for church music leaders have been around since at least 1940, when Southern Baptists held their inaugural Church Music Week at Ridgecrest Baptist Assembly in Ashville, North Carolina. Through the 1980s, most events targeted denominational markets, largely attracting church musicians who shared basic theological beliefs. Change began in the 1980s as events like Music California became popular, attracting worship leaders crossing denominational and theological lines. Today, there are no fewer than 30 national worship conferences featuring sermons, worship times, and breakout sessions led by popular educators, pastors, and worship leaders representing a wide range of theological perspectives. The largest, the National Worship Leader's Conference (NWLC), is sponsored by *Worship Leader* magazine and holds regional meetings throughout the year. Another example, Experience Conference, is held at Disney World's Contemporary Resort in Orlando, Florida. These types of events usually feature speakers that transcend denominational lines and utilize music from a number of different influences.

BOOKS

The theological breadth to which Christians are being exposed is demonstrated by the wide variety of inspirational books connecting with the market. The best-selling Christian books for November 2013, as compiled by the Evangelical Christian Publishers Association (ECPA), included authors from Joel Osteen and Joyce Meyer to Kyle Idleman, John Hagee, and Billy Graham. These titles included devotionals books, such as *Jesus Calling* by Sarah Young, those dealing with Christian living like *Emotions* by Charles Stanley, to *The Duck Commander Family* by Willie Robertson . . . and pretty much anything in between.

SOCIAL MEDIA

Facebook, Twitter, and blogs are platforms for people to express their opinions and expound on their theological belief system, regardless of the foundation of those systems. Unlike the publishing industry, there is no filter for social media. As a result, all variants of theological positions are represented online. Many popular church leaders embraced this technology as a means for staying connecting with their followers, often reaching thousands.

A BIBLICAL RESPONSE

So, is theology even important? In its Greek form, *theology* literally means "the study of God." Our theology is our view of God's sovereignty, sin, the Cross, and the Bible. Our theology impacts how we approach ministry, social issues, and missions. Therefore, a Bible-based theology is foundational in our roles as church leaders. Its role is exponentially expanded as planners of worship because the songs we select shape how others view God.

In a real sense, worship leaders are theological filters for our congregation. Have you ever had a miscue with your coffeemaker where the grounds spill over into the liquid? If so, you understand our role as worship leaders. Just as the filter separates the dregs from the drinkable liquid, as worship leaders we must insure that only solid theological truth is shared with our congregations. The Apostle Paul made this clear in his writing to Timothy:

> *If anyone teaches other doctrine and does not agree with the sound teaching of our Lord Jesus Christ and with the teaching that promotes godliness, he is conceited, understanding nothing, but has a sick interest in disputes and arguments over words. From these come envy, quarreling, slander, evil suspicions, and constant disagreement among people whose minds are depraved and deprived of the truth, who imagine that godliness is a way to material gain.*
> (1 Timothy 6:3–5)

In order to accomplish this with our congregations, worship leaders must intentionally build strong theological foundations. While resources such as conferences and books can be helpful, the standard of our theology must always be Scripture. In a culture that presents a plethora of views, opinions, and perspectives, a strong theological foundation allows us to discern truth from heresy, and protect the doctrinal differentiators that define our faith. When confident in our beliefs, "Then we will no longer be little children, tossed by the waves and blown around by every wind of teaching, by human cunning with cleverness in the techniques of deceit" (Ephesians 4:14).

WHAT NOW?

GATEKEEPERS OF TRUTH

As the music publishing industry shifted to downloadable products, many songs now go directly from the composer to the church's repertoire with little examination of theological content. With the added pressure to be on the cutting edge of the modern worship movement, many church leaders introduce new songs to their congregations without a passing glance at the text, much less a thorough review of the theological and doctrinal stances contained within. We must do better!

Church leaders must set a higher standard for songs used in worship services. Regardless of a song's popularity on Christian radio, or how many people say, "We should sing this," new songs must first being thoroughly evaluated for theological and doctrinal content before being introduced to our congregations.

Step 1: New song is given to team for review.

Step 2: Team meets to discuss the review, as well as sing the proposed song.

Step 3: Follow-up meeting to review any problems of content.

Step 4: Introduce song to congregation.

While a four-step process may appear cumbersome, it allows time to fully inspect the music and text to ensure the highest theological standards are upheld before sharing these with our congregations.

KNOW WHAT YOU BELIEVE

What are your beliefs on core doctrines of our faith? In reality, most popular worship songs focus on a limited number of doctrinal areas. When was the last time you heard a song on Christian education? Even so, we must be diligent in filtering new materials introduced to our congregations. To do this, we must clearly understand what we believe.

Most evangelical churches, denominations, Christian educational institutions, and parachurch organizations operate within a statement of faith clearly defining their view on key theological issues. The Southern Baptist Convention, for example, is guided by the *Baptist Faith and Message*, which serves as a summary statement of its defining beliefs. Similarly, Liberty University operates on a doctrinal statement that has guided the institution since its organization in 1971. With Scripture as our primary source, these types of documents are useful in clearly defining what we believe.

The following chart includes foundational doctrinal positions that can guide our song selection.[2] While the list is not comprehensive, it covers the primary areas expressed in worship.

TRINITY	• There is one God, infinite Spirit, Creator, and Sustainer of all things, who exists eternally in three persons, God the Father, God the Son, and God the Holy Spirit. • These three are one in essence but distinct in person and function.
GOD THE FATHER	• The Father is the first Person of the Trinity, and the source of all that God is and does. • From Him the Son is eternally generated, and from them, the Spirit eternally proceeds. • He is the designer of creation, the speaker of revelation, the author of redemption, and the sovereign of history.
GOD THE SON	• The Lord Jesus Christ is the second Person of the Trinity. • Eternally begotten from the Father, He is God. • He was conceived by the virgin Mary through a miracle of the Holy Spirit. • He lives forever as perfect God and perfect man, two distinct natures inseparably united in one person.
GOD THE SPIRIT	• The Holy Spirit is the third Person of the Trinity, proceeding from the Father and the Son, and equal in deity. • He is the giver of all life, active in the creating and ordering of the universe. • He is the agent of inspiration and the new birth. • He restrains sin and Satan. • He indwells and sanctifies all believers.
SCRIPTURE	• The Bible, both Old and New Testaments, though written by men, was supernaturally inspired by God so that all its words are the written true revelation of God. • It is inerrant in the originals and authoritative in all matters. • It is to be understood by all through the illumination of the Holy Spirit, its meaning determined by the historical, grammatical, and literary use of the author's language, comparing Scripture with Scripture.
SIN	• Adam, the first man, willfully disobeyed God, bringing sin and death into the world. • As a result, all persons are sinners from conception, which is evidenced in their willful acts of sin; and they are therefore subject to eternal punishment, under the just condemnation of a holy God.

ATONEMENT	• Jesus Christ offered Himself as a sacrifice by the appointment of the Father. • He fulfilled the demands of God by His obedient life, died on the Cross in full substitution and payment for the sins of all, was buried, and on the third day He arose physically and bodily from the dead. • He ascended into heaven where He now intercedes for all believers.
SALVATION	• Each person can be saved only through the work of Jesus Christ, through repentance of sin and by faith alone in Him as Savior. • The believer is declared righteous, born again by the Holy Spirit, turned from sin, and assured of heaven.
HOLY SPIRIT	• The Holy Spirit indwells all who are born again, conforming them to the likeness of Jesus Christ, a process completed only in heaven. • Every believer is responsible to live in obedience to the Word of God in separation from sin.
THE CHURCH	• A church is a local assembly of baptized believers, under the discipline of the Word of God and the lordship of Christ, organized to carry out the Commission to evangelize, to teach, and to administer the ordinances of believer's baptism and the Lord's Table. • Its offices are pastors and deacons, and it is self-governing. It functions through the ministry of gifts given by the Holy Spirit to each believer.
CHRIST'S RETURN	• The return of Christ for all believers is imminent. • It will be followed by seven years of great tribulation, and then the coming of Christ to establish His earthly kingdom for a thousand years. • The unsaved will then be raised and judged according to their works and separated forever from God in hell. The saved, having been raised, will live forever in heaven in fellowship with God.

IMPORTANCE OF THEOLOGICAL EDUCATION

As churches placed heavier emphasis on musical skills, and some seminaries refused to acknowledge these skills were even needed, a vacuum developed leaving many worship leaders with weak theological foundations. To remedy this problem, churches, as well as those called to the worship ministry, must rediscover the importance of a solid theological education.

Seminaries and Christian colleges are finally acknowledging the local worship culture shifts, and their approaches to educating worship students are beginning to change to reflect actual market needs. At the same time, churches must insist that worship pastors have solid theological education from Christian colleges or seminaries. Online education in worship studies has removed many obstacles that once made this type of education a challenge. It is past time to raise the standard of theological truth.

CONCLUSION

While the modern worship movement ushered in many positive changes, including a renewed focus on worship and a fresh connection with an entire generation of young Christians, the importance of theological education for those leading worship became a casualty. Many worship leaders developed a convergent theological system influenced by any number of forces, including media, Pentecostalism, Reformed theology, and the CCM industry. Since 1990, many young worship leaders took the buffet approach (either intentionally or unintentionally), handpicking theological points from varying influences to form their own belief systems. At best, the result was theological illiteracy and, at worse, a convoluted mess.

This melting pot of influences resulted in many churches, even those with strong denominational identities, losing many of the theological distinctiveness that defined them for generations. While traditionalism in and of itself is not good, its parameters defined by doctrine and theology are indispensable. After all, should a Southern Baptist church be identical to an Assemblies of God congregation? Likewise, should a Methodist congregation give up core doctrinal beliefs based on the music used in worship? Over the next decade, churches must make a renewed effort to filter the songs used in worship because of their role in shaping the way we believe. Somewhere a balance exists between four stanzas of a Charles Wesley hymn and the latest Jesus-is-my-best-friend worship song. For the sake of our churches, we need to find it!

CHAPTER 8

Worship Leader, Version 2.0:

THE LOSS OF THE WORSHIP PASTOR AS A LIFELONG CALLING

It is the proverbial elephant in the room: aging worship leaders viewed with disdain in the local church. Granted, this attitude is seldom publically expressed, but it is still there. After all, can a worship leader in their 40s or 50s really connect with the modern worship culture? The most common answer is no. The result: experienced worship pastors are being unceremoniously dumped and replaced with newer, trendier models. The implications of this attitude have placed the lifelong calling as worship pastor in peril.

The role of the worship pastor is a relatively recent historical development. As men returned from battle following World War II, many did so with a renewed zeal for Christ that resulted in a dramatic increase in church attendance. Since the 1930s, Southern Baptist leaders had decried the state of music in their churches. The postwar momentum created an opportunity for leaders such as I. E. Reynolds (Southwestern Baptist Theological Seminary), E. O. Sellers (New Orleans Baptist Theological Seminary), and B. B. McKinney (Baptist Sunday School Board) to lead an effort to improve the quality of church music. This focus launched numerous schools of music and state church music departments, while at the same time gave birth to an entirely new vocational ministry position: the vocational worship pastor.

In the years following 1945, the role as worship pastor experienced nuanced changes, primarily focused on the growth of choirs, the need for stronger administrative skills, and a growing requirement for large-scale productions. The core musical requirements, however, remained largely unchanged. As a result, many worship pastors spent their entire ministerial careers as the primary worship leader, some serving the same church for decades. Gerald Ray (First Baptist Church, Houston, TX), Larry Black (First Baptist Church, Jackson, MS), and Jim Whitmire (Bellevue Baptist Church, Cordova, TN) are excellent examples of men who, through strong relationships and creative vision, served their churches with distinction. Over the past ten years, however, things have changed. The prospects of the modern worship pastor remaining in the same role until retirement are at best minimal, and at worse, highly unlikely.

There are two primary factors contributing to this change. First, the modern worship renewal ushered in new skill requirements in the areas of contemporary Christian music and technology. Many worship pastors trained prior to 1990 do not have these skills due to breakdowns in seminary and Christian college education for worship pastors. Second, because of a desire to connect with culture, a growing number of churches intentionally target younger leaders to be the "face" of the worship service. This often results in retirement or reassignment, sometimes at the worship pastor's initiative, other times not.

Another challenge is the definition of *aging* has changed, especially within the context of worship ministry. Most worship pastors begin their ministries with the basic assumption they will lead worship until retirement. The factors discussed above, however, have challenged that assumption. While most worship pastors expect, and even anticipate, retirement when they reach the golden years, many worship pastors now face this reality much younger. Because they have a narrow and specialized skill set, many have few options moving forward.

WHAT GOES AROUND

In the race to "young up" the platform and bring energy to their services, many churches target worship leaders fresh out of college. With churches dangling ministry positions in front of them like carrots on a stick, many young worship leaders short-circuit their education and skill development in favor of regular employment. When faced with the options of graduate school or a paying job, the temptation is often too great! Unfortunately, in 20 years many of the churches hiring the "youngest and best" to lead worship, will be searching for the "younger and better" to replace them. Based on the effects of time, the old version will not fit the bill.

This reality was expressed in a blog post by Zac Hicks, pastor of worship at Coral Ridge Presbyterian Church in Fort Lauderdale, Florida, on June 6, 2011 (zachicks.com), when he wrote:

> I had a recent phone conversation with a worship leader friend of mine who leads music on the other side of the country. In a candid moment, we were both expressing concerns about the longevity of our jobs as local church music leaders. We wondered whether, in ten to fifteen years, we would be viewed as out-of-date, irrelevant, washed up, and cheesy—one of those old guys trying to look and act young. Ultimately, we questioned whether we would be as effective in doing our task once we started "looking old." ...
>
> Though I've never heard it from a single one of them, I'd bet that every twentysomething who's been a worship leader for more than a year has had the thought, "What happens when I get older?" (Implication: I have to do something different, because this can't work.)

Every week we receive phone calls from experienced worship pastors, either being forced out of their roles, or concerned about their ability to survive long term. Some feel angry, hurt, or betrayed; most are simply scared.

THE LOSS OF A LIFELONG CALLING

In a 2011 article for *The Christian Post* (christianpost.com), entitled "Church Staff: Some Observations," Thom S. Rainer highlighted a trend that shows about four percent of church staff is terminated each year. This translates to 1 in 25 staff members, a termination rate much higher than that of senior pastors which stands at 1.5 percent (1 in 67). While this research does not deal exclusively with the position of worship pastor, anecdotal evidence suggests the move to younger worship leaders is part of this trend.

It should be noted that there are situations when termination is the right course of action. Worship pastors who are incompetent (musically and/or relationally), lazy, resist change, or refuse to expand needed skill sets must not be allowed to hide in the bushes and hinder the vision of the church. In those cases, church leaders must have the courage to make the right decision. Decisions to terminate are never easy. For the sake of the gospel, sometimes they are needed.

Another way churches deal with aging worship pastors is by reassigning them to other ministry roles. Often times this is more politically palatable and allows continuing service to the church. Some worship pastors welcome the reassignments, often because they feel ill equipped to handle the changing worship culture or they are simply burned out. Others begrudgingly make the shift but do so with a sense of bitterness and resentment. There are countless examples of former worship pastors who now serve in senior adult, pastoral care, or executive pastor roles with varying degrees of success.

In some cases, worship pastors simply give up. Many are tired of fighting battles over music style. Others feel they are no longer relevant to the modern worship culture. Whatever the reasons, thousands each year shift to new careers late in their ministries. Real estate offices, insurance agencies, car dealerships, and classrooms are filled with former worship pastors who have moved on to other vocational options. Because of narrow skill sets, however, even these transitions can be difficult.

THE BENEFITS OF EXPERIENCE

Experienced worship pastors can bring much to the table regarding the heritage and life experiences of a church family.

- They remember significant celebrations and tragedies in the lives of church members.
- They have celebrated victories and lamented losses, both in their ministry area and churchwide.
- They have an awareness of potential roadblocks that can hinder progress.
- The bring a sense of perspective in the midst of a rapidly changing culture,
- They can serve as catalyst for consensus in moving forward.

This collective information, sometimes referred to as institutional memory, is hugely beneficial for churches as they cast vision, redefine goals, and develop strategies, while simultaneously trying to balance issues of heritage and tradition. Forcing staff changes prematurely can upset this balance and leave church leadership with no understanding of the underlying identity of the congregation. As churches work through questions of vision and purpose, it helps to know from whence we came. Experience can potentially provide this perspective.

In Acts 20, Paul utilized a biblical version of institutional memory as he prepared to go to Jerusalem. In this passage he calls together the leaders of the church at Ephesus and outlines benchmarks that will strengthen him for an uncertain journey:

> *Now from Miletus, he sent to Ephesus and called for the elders of the church. And when they came to him, he said to them: "You know, from the first day I set foot in Asia, how I was with you the whole time—serving the Lord with all humility, with tears, and with the trials that came to me through the plots of the Jews—and that I did not shrink back from proclaiming to you anything that was profitable or from teaching it to you in public and from house to house. I testified to both Jews and Greeks about repentance toward God and faith in our Lord Jesus.*
>
> *And now I am on my way to Jerusalem, bound in my spirit, not knowing what I will encounter there, except that in*

town after town the Holy Spirit testifies to me that chains and afflictions are waiting for me. But I count my life of no value to myself, so that I may finish my course and the ministry I received from the Lord Jesus, to testify to the gospel of God's grace.

(vv. 17–24)

As the Ephesians experienced, supportive worship pastors remember where we have been and can help us get to where we are going. We simply have to allow them to take the journey with us.

The success of our ministries is largely dependent on our ability to build meaningful relationships. Experienced worship pastors have built-in relational connections that can help mobilize a church for new era. In many churches, up to 20 percent of a congregation can be directly involved with the worship ministry. These ministries often are characterized by meaningful relationships. Over the years, experienced worship pastors have:

- visited church members in the hospital;
- preached weddings and funerals;
- led students to the Lord on missions trips and choir tours;
- baptized children who made professions of faith at Vacation Bible School; and,
- led the church family in meaningful time of worship and celebration.

These relationships are real and must not be approached flippantly. Church leaders must understand the significance of these relational ties and exercise great caution before severing them.

A BIBLICAL RESPONSE

Prior to the late 1960s aging and life experience were viewed differently by the culture. Older people were afforded a sense of honor and respect because of their age, often serving as teachers, spiritual advisers, and mentors. This is still true in some areas of our culture. The academic and health-care communities place added value on individuals with extensive experience. (When was the last time you requested a surgeon straight out of medical school?) This is not necessarily the case in churches.

Scripture has a different model. We are commanded to honor our elders, especially those who have spiritual authority over us. The following passages demonstrate some of the attitudes we are to have in regards to those with life experience:

♩= **Leviticus 19:32**—"You are to rise in the presence of the elderly and honor the old. Fear your God; I am Yahweh."

♩= **Titus 2:2**—"Older men are to be level headed, worthy of respect, sensible, and sound in faith, love, and endurance."

♩= **1 Timothy 5:1**—"Do not rebuke an older man, but exhort him as a father, younger men as brothers."

♩= **Proverbs 20:29**—"The glory of young men is their strength, and the splendor of old men is gray hair."

Scripture teaches experience is a good thing! It also carries strong admonitions for those who claim that title: levelheaded, worthy of respect, sensible, and sound in faith, love, and endurance. When experienced worship leaders display those characteristics, their value to the vision and mission of our churches is incredible.

𝄢 WHAT NOW?

Although the dominant trend is toward younger worship leaders, it does not have to be an "all or nothing" scenario. Our churches need passion and energy, while balancing wisdom and influence. There is room on the platform for both! Below are suggestions to help churches and experienced worship pastors refocus their hearts and minds as we move into the years ahead.

FOCUS ON CALLING, NOT POSITION

How do you define your ministry? Do you view yourself as a musician or pastor? Does your joy in ministry come from your official role? These are important questions we must ask in order to accurately understand our calling to ministry. We must remember our first priority is to love God with our entire being. This can be done regardless of the title we hold or roles we fill within the life of our church. The rest is about relationships . . . we ultimately are in the people business! Based on the research below, many ministers do not understand this.

Each month some 1,500 Protestant and evangelical ministers leave the ministry. Al Mohler, president of Southern Baptist Theological Seminary, suggested there are two primary reasons for this in a talk called "Why Do Pastors Leave the Ministry" (albertmohler.com): (1) Either the person has not been called, or (2) they have a faulty understanding of ministry. Mohler goes on to say, "If you know *who* called you and you know *what* you've been called to do, then you *won't* quit!"

Often our expectations and understanding of ministry are skewed. Placing an unhealthy emphasis on performance has encouraged many worship leaders to view their role as a performer, artist, or professional musician. As a result, the first time an irate church member accosts them over music selection, they head for the exit. Our clear understanding of our calling is critical because it keeps us from quitting when things get hard.

A major part of the challenge is that our expectations are inaccurate. Remember, performers are idolized . . . followers of Christ are crucified. That being true, should we as worship leaders expect any different treatment than Christ? To be effective in our role as worship pastors we must die to self, which Paul emphasized in Galatians 2:19–20 when he said, "I have been crucified with Christ and I no longer live, but Christ lives in me." Dying to self is not easy, especially for those accustomed to being the out-front leaders. At the end of the day, however, our calling transcends individual interests and professional goals. We are called to be ministers, not musicians, and must lay ambition and skill at the foot of the Cross. God calls us to share His love and the message of salvation to a lost world. The roles we fill to accomplish this task must be secondary if we are to reach our culture for Christ.

UNDERSTAND YOUR ROLE IN SHARED MINISTRY
While most churches still have positions labeled "senior pastor" and

"worship pastor" (or some variant thereof), the program-based model of church staffing is disappearing. According to Thom Rainer:

> The responsibilities and names of church staff positions are incredibly diverse. When churches were largely program driven, they would offer [sic] call or hire staff according to the program. Thus a music minister was hired for the music program. An educational minister was brought on staff to oversee the educational program. And a youth minister was added for youth programs. Though those positions still exist, program oversight is no longer the primary motivator for adding many staff members.

Understanding this shift is critical for those called to worship ministry. The days of the staff musician, who primarily handled choirs, orchestras, and seasonal productions, are gone. The new model integrates music with worship, discipleship, evangelism, and missions.

This has enormous implications for those serving local churches. In the past, ministry areas functioned independently, often with music, education, and missions building their own little kingdoms. As an example, after joining the staff in one of the churches we served, we learned the student ministry was not allowed to use microphones because they "belonged" to the music ministry (for the record, this was corrected very quickly). In another situation student choir workers were engaged in battles over control of student music. These types of attitudes are unhealthy, unbiblical, and thankfully no longer acceptable.

In recent years some progress was made. Staff teams became comfortable with collaborative approaches that placed related ministries at the same table. In these settings, the children's ministry had equal input into children's music, and the student ministry influenced the location of student choir missions trips. While this was a marked improvement over the "little kingdoms" approach, it still fell short of the shared ministry model.

The new model must be a team process in which planning and collaboration expands beyond related ministries to reflect *intergenerational connection*. As family ministry explodes, an emerging trend driven by the millennials, all the ministries of the church must become intergenerational rather than age-segregated. Staff teams must work together to design programming and strategies that reflect vision and purpose. In a shared ministry model:

- collegiate ministry influences how seasonal musical productions are designed;
- pastors leading buster ministries partner in planning strategies related to children's worship;
- ministry-specific programming, though important, is driven by its connection to evangelism and missions; and
- ministry areas, fueled by a desire for deeper teaching, are expected to integrate discipleship and biblical teaching into specific approaches.

This will require the worship pastor and his team to cross dividing lines that have been in place far too long. One way to accomplish this is through *interlocking meetings*, in which staff members from different areas meet together to ensure everyone is working in partnership.

This move to a shared ministry approach changes the way the worship pastor functions. While the most visible role remains leading the church family in worship, spiritual characteristics, such as personal evangelism and discipleship, take on increased importance. Leadership and managerial skills become equally important, focusing on team building, communication, negotiation, and conflict management. These skills are foundational in unifying diverse teams, often with competing interests, and are basic requirements in a shared ministry model.

Building consensus is difficult work, but the end result makes the effort worthwhile. Because worship intersects with so many parts of church life, the twenty-first-century worship pastor will be pivotal in building synergy for a shared ministry model.

EMBRACE THE ROLE OF MENTOR

Proverbs 27:17 reminds us that, "Iron sharpens iron, and one man sharpens another." As young worship leaders flood the church market, experienced worship pastors must create opportunities to build strong mentoring relationships. Not only do these relationships provide a direct connection to the modern worship culture, they create opportunities to shape the next generation of worship leaders.

It is not only about mentoring musicians. Experienced worship pastors must develop mentoring relationships with younger ministers in other ministry areas. This builds deep and meaningful staff relationships and allows the worship pastor to connect with the heart and passion of fellow team members. Peter wrote about how Philip modeled a mentoring relationship for us in Acts 8:27–31:

> There was an Ethiopian man, a eunuch and high official of Candace, queen of the Ethiopians, who was in charge of her entire treasury. He had come to worship in Jerusalem and was sitting in his chariot on his way home, reading the prophet Isaiah aloud.
>
> The Spirit told Philip, "Go and join that chariot."
>
> When Philip ran up to it, he heard him reading the prophet Isaiah, and said, "Do you understand what you're reading?"
>
> "How can I," he said, "unless someone guides me?" So he invited Philip to come up and sit with him.

The modern church culture is complex and presents numerous challenges. These are compounded for younger ministers who at times can be overwhelmed and frustrated with ministry situations and relational conflict. Sometimes they need advice, while other times they simply need a friend. By intentionally building mentoring relationship, worship pastors can encourage, disciple, and influence worship for years to come. The vast majority of younger ministers desire to grow spiritually and professionally.

In some ways they are asking the same question as the Ethiopian: "How can I, unless someone guides me?" As experienced worship pastors, we must be willing to fill that role.

DEVELOP MULTIGENERATIONAL TEAM MODELS

A basic axiom of management is "hire to your weaknesses." While growing older is not necessarily a weakness, worship pastors must commit to shape teams around a multigenerational identity. This is true for paid staff as well as volunteer leadership. As churches adjust to a growing emphasis on intergenerational ministry, our leadership teams must reflect this as well.

Many of the arguments supporting multigenerational worship also apply to staff philosophies. Age diverse teams bring unique perspectives to our ministry and challenge us to think outside of the box. In order to stay creatively fresh, we need this. If everyone on your team is close to your age, then you have a problem!

♩=♩♪

Short-Circuited Education—A Parable

Twenty years ago Chuck was the coolest kid on campus. Blessed with good looks and a charismatic personality, he also was the lead singer and guitarist for the most popular band on campus. Chuck had a contagious love of Jesus, and he his band regularly led church youth rallies and Disciple Now weekends all across the state. As he approached his senior year in college, a cutting-edge church in his college town needed a worship leader, and Chuck was the obvious choice. Although he planned on going to seminary to continue his education, the offer was too good to pass.

Now things are different. Although Chuck and his pastor have worked together for two decades, things are feeling tense between them. The church had always targeted the student population, but several months back the pastor starting hinting that a younger worship leader might help them bridge the gap to that target group. The official word came today: a transition was coming in six months.

Chuck begins calling pastor friends to see if there are any ministry positions available that might be a good fit. While the responses are cordial and encouraging, in his spirit Chuck knows he is in trouble. Those churches are looking for younger worship leaders as well. His worship leader friends are no help either. Many of them are in the same position! In a desperate attempt to avoid relocating his wife and two kids, Chuck contacts his alma mater across town to see if there might be a teaching position available. After all, with his experience and connection with the community he could bring a practical perspective to the classroom. Unfortunately, a bachelor's degree in general studies does not give him the credentials to teach on the college level. Options are quickly running out and Chuck is scared.

♫=♩♪

This scenario is played out weekly by worship leaders across the United States. As these words are being written, there are more than 30 names in a "Prospective Faculty" file representing worship pastors who have contacted the Center for Music and Worship at Liberty University for teaching positions. None of them have the basic educational requirements to even be considered. While they bring enormous practical experience to the table, their lack of academic preparation prevents them from teaching at the collegiate level.

We have two important recommendations regarding academic preparation. First, if you are called to be a worship pastor, then pursue the highest level of training possible. Second, if you are serving as a worship pastor and did not get adequate education, enroll in a worship degree program as soon as possible! While this may seem blunt, it is true. Education will not allow you to keep a position, or even get you the job, but it will open doors that otherwise would be closed. In our technology-driven culture, there are no good excuses to put off this decision. Worship pastors have access to Bible-based education through various formats, including residential and online degree programs.

So what is adequate education for a worship pastor? It depends on the context of your ministry and what you feel called to do. With that understanding, if you are called to full-time ministry as a worship pastor, a master's degree in worship studies, or its equivalent, should be the goal. This allows for advanced studies in worship and theology, sharpens your skills as a worship leader, and will create opportunities when unexpected life and ministry events occur . . . and they will occur. Err on the side of education. We can give you a list of names of individuals who wish they had!

BROADEN INFLUENCE ACROSS GENERATIONAL LINES

In order to connect with other generations, we must spend time with them! This sounds simple, but it is not as easy as you might think. There is a reason it is called a generation gap. We have different attitudes, interests, and viewpoints. We dress differently, talk differently, entertain ourselves differently, and according to Sam Rainer, in the article "10 (Unexpected) Church Trends to Surface by 2020" (churchleaders.com), there "is just as large a generation gap between the Boomers and the Greatest Generation as there is between Boomers and their children." Finding opportunities for shared experiences takes intentionality and effort.

One popular preacher calls this the "spiritual gift of hanging out." Simple things like attending student ministry events or participating in a family missions project allows people to connect with you outside the church environment. Attending Little League games or programs at local schools demonstrates to students that you care about them and the things in which they are involved. Teaching a class at a local college or speaking at a local civic club allows you to meet potential ministry members outside you immediate sphere of influence. The opportunities are almost limitless; it is just a matter of making it a priority in your ministry.

WHAT SEASON IS IT?

Ecclesiastes 3:1 reminds us, "There is an occasion for everything, and a time for every activity under heaven." The question is, Do you know what season you are in? As worship pastors we must pray for discernment so we can honestly evaluate our ministries. Some questions to ponder include:

- Am I still effective in my current role?
- Do volunteers and staff connect with my leadership?
- When I awake is there a sense of excitement about responsibilities for the day?
- Am I enlisting a ministry team that reflects our community in age and focus?
- Do I intentionally mentor younger ministers, or am I threatened by their presence?
- Is this a job or a passion?
- Is there another role that is a better fit?

Determining if a season of life is over can be a difficult and traumatic process. In the end, the Holy Spirit must guide our thoughts and decisions. Remember, it is the call of God on our life that drives us, not our role, position or title.

CONCLUSION

Beginning in the mid-1940s, a calling as worship pastor was recognized by churches as an important part of ministry to local congregations. For the next 60 years, hundreds of church musicians responded to this call, many serving churches their entire ministries. Beginning around 2005, however, that started to change. As churches began attempting to reach the millennials, worship leaders, some as young as 40 or 50, were deemed too old and were terminated, reassigned, or forced to retire . . . primarily because of age. These staffing decisions often resulted in a loss of institutional memory, important relational connections, and ministry wisdom. Unfortunately, many of the replaced worship pastors had few options because of minimal education and narrow skill sets. As we move into the next decade we must find better options.

The role of the worship pastor is changing. Gone are the days of the staff musician who primarily led choirs and orchestra. While leading worship will remain the most visible role, worship pastors must focus on pastoral care, missions, and discipleship. As part of a shared ministry model, multigenerational teams must be developed to reflect the composition of our congregations, and worship pastors must be intentional in mentoring and fostering relationships that transcend generational boundaries. While our primary role for decades was leading music, worship, discipleship, evangelism, and missions must now be the defining characteristics.

The next ten years will be significant for those called to serve local churches as worship pastors because if the worship pastor's role is not redefined based on calling, rather than music, the fastest growing segment of the modern worship culture will most likely be former worship pastors. At that point, it will become a job relegated to 20- or 30-somethings, and an important lifelong calling will be irretrievably lost.

CHAPTER 9

Multisensory Overload:

WORSHIP IN A TECHNOLOGY-DRIVEN CULTURE

An amazing invention— but who would ever want to use one?
—President Rutherford B. Hayes, referring to the telephone

Computers, email, smartphones, tablets, social media—in many ways technology defines our culture. Those of us who used typewriters for college papers while armed with a freshly purchased bottle of correction fluid find computers as a way of life a significant blessing. Many others, however, have never seen such an antique machine (with the possible exception of the one on display at the National Museum of American History in Washington, DC) and have no concept of just how far word-processing technology has come. Countless technological advances have improved the quality of our lives. With these advances, however, come challenges.

Throughout history, technology has always influenced the church. The first book ever published—in 1440, when Johannes Gutenberg invented a moveable-type printing press—was the Bible. The events that followed are even more significant. In 1517, some 77 years later, Martin Luther nailed his *Ninety-Five Theses* to the door of the Wittenberg Church, igniting the Protestant Reformation, which swept across Europe and changed the face of Christianity. It is difficult to imagine how the Protestant Reformation could have happened absent Gutenberg's invention, which placed the Bible in the hands of common people and helped spread the underlying ideals.

Other technological innovations have similarly impacted the church. Any minister receiving a late-night telephone call to discuss church business can thank a gentleman by the name of Alexander Graham Bell. Innovation often prompted major shifts in philosophy. For example, Henry Ford's automobile directly influenced the rise of consumerism. With personal transportation options more accessible, people, often influenced by their personal preferences, could choose where to attend church. Mimeograph machines and later digital copiers produced orders of service and teaching materials. Air conditioning impacted times and length of services. The invention of radio and television launched mass evangelism in ways never imagined in the early decades of the twentieth century. Examples of technological connections with the church are countless, but the implications are clear: technology shapes church practice.

While technology really is a tool, it is not neutral. Just as speakers or musicians frame the content of their sermons or songs within the context of their personal beliefs and preferences, particular applications of technology shape and influence how people perceive the message delivered through a specific medium. In our effort to creatively engage our culture, we must be careful the mode of delivery does not mask the message.

Several years ago, a church we served planned a student-led worship night featuring student worship leaders, choirs, and a band. Leading up to the event, we learned the student pastor planned to rappel from the attic as the lead in to his sermon. While this maneuver (if he survived it) would have been attention grabbing, he had a major problem: his preaching skills were, at best, limited. Our advice to him was, "If you are using something that spectacular as an introduction, you better be able to follow it up!" While his intentions were great, the focus was wrong. The use of creativity and innovation is not wrong. Churches across the world effectively use a wide variety of tools and experiences to engage people in worship, including elaborate props, multimedia experiences and creative sermon introductions (yes, rappelling *can* be effective). The challenge, though, is when the lines between entertainment and worship become blurred. Ephesians 4:14 reminds us of the importance of focusing on solid, biblical teaching: "Then we will no longer be little children, tossed by the waves and blown around by every wind of teaching, by human cunning with cleverness in the techniques of deceit." Technology can be a great ally in sharing the story of God's love for mankind, but we must insure our methods never obscure the message.

IT'S A JUNGLE OUT THERE

Because of the overwhelming variety of technology available, it is virtually impossible to stay current on every new development or emerging trend. There are three specific advancements, however, which exert enormous influence in our culture and are forcing churches to struggle with how to integrate them into the life of the church: the Internet, cell phones, and social media.

INTERNET

In the early 1990s watching movies or reading books online seemed like a concept for a science fiction movie. Today, these activities are part of everyday life. According to research conducted by Pew Research Center (pewinternet.org) in May 2013, 85 percent of American adults use the Internet. Believe it or not, this usage is not limited to just the younger generations. More than half of adults over the age of 65 use the Internet or email on a regular basis.

The Internet opened countless options for church use in the areas of promotion, outreach, and mass evangelism. Live streaming, sermon archives, and online registrations are now the norm for many churches. Seventy-eight percent of churches have websites, often the first point of contact for families exploring possible church homes. The Southern Baptist Convention offers assistance to churches through a rudimentary website called ChurchSearch (sbc.net/churchsearch). Even so, churches grossly underutilize the Internet's potential. According to LifeWay Research, while an overwhelming number of churches have a website, less than half use them for interactive purposes such as gathering and distributing prayer requests or online event registration. An "information only" church website substantially limits the potential impact for that church.

CELL PHONES

It is hard to imagine life without cell phones. Most Americans agree since 91 percent own one. Pay telephones, previously a common fixture of street corners, are long gone. Today your smartphone controls your calendar, schedules dinner reservations, and serves as your personal assistant while allowing you to verbally interact with others. As long as we are close to a cell tower or connected to Wi-Fi, we can track the location of our children (Pew Research also found that 78 percent of teenagers have a cell phone, with nearly half of those being smartphones), purchase birthday presents, download apps, or send photos to friends and family. Many are so con-nected to their phones that they feel "exposed" if it is not within literally within reach. Even at night, two-thirds of Americans sleep with them next to their beds!

Cell phones provide around-the-clock access to family and friends. Yet, these same tools also create problems including limited attention spans, texting while driving, and technology addiction. These tools can create problems for pastors and preachers who quote statistics and stories of dubious authenticity. In the twenty-first century, many preachers are quickly called out for preaching someone else's sermon! Next time you are in a restaurant, observe other people (after putting away your own phone) to see how many are texting or checking email. Another interesting exer-cise is to count the number of folks talking while driving who pass by as you wait out a stoplight! We simply cannot seem to put them down. Pew researchers tell us the average text messaging user sends or receives 41.5

messages every day. As expected, the youngest adults (those between the ages of 18 and 24) rely heavily on this form of communication, sending or receiving an average of 109.5 text messages per day (more than 3,200 messages per month).

As smartphones and similar devices continue to advance and users become increasingly dependent, the impact of this trend on churches will expand exponentially. As of May 2013, 63 percent adult cell owners access the Internet on their phones. Mobile devices, including smartphones, are now the primary tool for online shopping, bill payments, social media, and staying connected with their jobs.

SOCIAL MEDIA

Social media influences many areas of our lives, with users relying on Facebook and Twitter to connect with family and friends, as well as obtain information about social and world events. In fact, the Pew Research Center's Journalism Project (journalism.org) discovered that 30 percent of the US population now turns to Facebook as a source for news.

While the vast majority is not yet turning off their favorite news channel in favor of social media, its role in everyday life is rapidly increasing. These platforms allow us to connect with old friends, respond to political and world events, and form broader networks than ever before possible. If used effectively, social media effectively shrinks large communities into smaller groups, a huge incentive for churches and ministries needing to connect with members and prospects. Most church members are already proficient in social media: 66 percent of adult Internet users belong to a social network (including 86 percent of those ages 18–29), with 48 percent using the sites on a daily basis.[1]

THE GOOD, THE BAD, AND THE UGLY

Technological advances, like most things, potentially have both positive and negative impact. A key benefit influenced by technological innovation is the ability to communicate, regardless of location or distance. In a real sense, technology broke down physical and geographical barriers allowing most people to take care of work-related issues from anywhere. Technological advances, including the Internet, led to the advent of online education, making opportunities to pursue college, graduate, or terminal education readily accessible. We would be remiss if we did not mention the Internet's impact on relationships: Pew Research reports that more than one-third of those "single and looking" reported using an online dating site or dating app. With the positives, however, negative impacts on society have evolved.

INTERNET ADDICTION

How often do you check your email? Do you waste large amounts of time surfing the Internet? Do you experience withdrawals if your phone it is not in your possession? If so, you are not alone. The problem of Internet addiction was officially recognized by the American Psychiatric Association in the May 2013 edition of their *Diagnostic and Statistical Manual of Mental Health Disorders* (DSM-5). These mental health experts continue their studies of Internet addictions among Americans, especially among young people.

In recent years a great percentage of Americans described themselves as being addicted to the Internet. This disorder, which includes addictions to text messaging and gaming, is characterized by symptoms similar to other addictions:

- Withdrawal symptoms
- A need to spend increasing amounts of time engaged in Internet activities
- Unsuccessful attempts to control Internet use
- Continued excessive Internet use despite knowledge of negative psychosocial problems
- Loss of interests, previous hobbies, and entertainment as a result of, and with the exception of Internet use
- Use of the Internet to escape or relieve depression
- Deception of family members, therapists, or others regarding the amount of Internet use

- Jeopardized or lost a significant relationship, job, or educational or career opportunity because of Internet use.

While most check email on a regular basis, some report doing so over and over again all day. In one example, a respondent admitted to checking and replying to her email even at 3:00 a.m.[2]

SOCIAL ISOLATION

Technology based tools is a two-edged sword in relationship building: we can have large number of connections and still be isolated from meaningful relationships. Having 2,000 friends on Facebook does not translate into meaningful relationships. Regular emails, text messages, or chat sessions fall into the same category. Granted, we are connecting with more people, but at what level?

POOR INTERPERSONAL COMMUNICATION SKILLS

Technology addiction research is relatively new, but growing evidence exists that one of the negative impacts is weakened interpersonal communication skills. While glued to our computers, PDAs, tablets, and smartphones, we risk losing our ability to understand nonverbal communication of others such as interpreting of body language and facial expressions. If not careful, our ability to intelligently confront issues, counsel others, deal with conflict, and offer solutions may default to responses of 140 characters or less. Today, people commonly resign jobs, deliver difficult work-related information, and end dating relationships via email or text messages. Interpersonal communication skills are imperative for church leaders. In many cases, the ability to interact face-to-face with others has been a casualty of modern technology.

INFLUENCE ON FAMILY

Technology impacts how families communicate, as well as the manner in which they develop interpersonal relationships. As part of a 2011 Barna Group (barna.org) study, parents and teens (ages 11–17) from the same households were interviewed to identify the influence of technology on their families. This research highlighted several key findings:

- Parents are just as dependent as teens and tweens.
- Parent use technology and media to nearly the same degree as their 11- to 17-year-olds.
- Parents watch just as much television and movies, use the Internet for as many minutes per day, and spend more time on the telephone and emailing than do their tweens and teenaged children.
- Nearly a two-to-one ratio of parents viewed technology as making their family life better rather than worse (32 percent to 18 percent). Most describe the influence as neutral (51 percent).
- Most families welcome technology and media with open arms, rather than with suspicion. One of the reasons may be that many families use technology, including television, movies, and video games, as a shared experience.
- One out of three parents and nearly half of 11- to 17-year-olds say there are no specific times when they "make the choice to disconnect from or turn off technology so they can have a break from it." And those who take such breaks tend to be driven by convenience rather than intention.
- For example, only 10 percent of parents and 6 percent of teenagers say they try to take off one day a week from their digital usage.
- Nearly half of both parents and teens said they emailed, texted, or talked on the phone while eating in the last week.
- Most parents and tweens/teens have not received teaching in a church, religious setting, or public forum (such as a school) concerning how families can best use media, entertainment, or technology.

Without boundaries, technology can have a direct and negative impact on families. David Kinnaman, president of Barna Group, addressed this by saying:

> Technology is shaping family interactions in unprecedented ways, but we seem to lack a strategic commitment

to the stewardship of technology. The Christian community needs a better, more holistic understanding of how to manage existing and coming technological advances. Parents, tweens and teens need more coaching and input in order to face the countless choices they make regarding how technology affects their attention, interests, talents and resources.

🎼 A BIBLICAL RESPONSE

So, is technology referenced in the Bible? The answer might surprise you. In addition to being the inspired Word of God, Scripture traces the development of the human race. The Bible is an accurate reflection of history, thus advances in technology can be seen throughout its pages. One of the early examples of God-directed use of technology occurs relative to the flood. If you recall, God instructed Noah to construct an exceptionally elaborate boat.

> *Make yourself an ark of gopher wood. Make rooms in the ark, and cover it with pitch inside and outside. This is how you are to make it: The ark will be 450 feet long, 75 feet wide, and 45 feet high. You are to make a roof, finishing the sides of the ark to within 18 inches of the roof. You are to put a door in the side of the ark. Make it with lower, middle, and upper decks.*
> (Genesis 6:14–16)

If a boat of this magnitude, constructed to these specifics, is not extensive applications of technology, then what is? The Bible is filled with examples of technological application: the building of the temple required advanced technology in design, engineering and construction, as did Nehemiah's rebuilding of the walls of Jerusalem. David creatively used a slingshot to slay Goliath. Even Jesus used a tool when preaching the parable of the sower in Matthew 13: because of the crowds gathered to hear Him, He used a boat, probably the latest generation and most advanced fishing vessel of the day, as a makeshift platform and moved out on the water for amplification purposes.

TOWARDS THE GREAT COMMISSION

Technology played a significant role as churches pursued obedience to the Great Commission. From Billy Graham's groundbreaking crusades to the international use of the *Jesus* film (viewed approximately more than 6 billion times, per jesusfilm.org), technological advances enabled our taking the gospel to the nations. One organization, Faith Comes by Hearing (faithcomesbyhearing.com), uses smartphones and tablets, preloaded with versions of the Bible, as a platform to get Scripture into closed nations. While methodologies vary, the words of Jesus are very clear:

> *Go, therefore, and make disciples of all nations, baptizing them in the name of the Father and of the Son and of the Holy Spirit, teaching them to observe everything I have commanded you. And remember, I am with you always, to the end of the age.*
>
> (Matthew 28:19–20)

Remember: technology is a tool, a means to an end. It should not define our churches. Instead, its biblical role is as a tool with a myriad of options for our use in sharing the love of Christ to a world in desperate need of Him. As Paul reminded us in 1 Corinthians 9:22, "I have become all things to all people, so that I may by every possible means save some."

 WHAT NOW?
IT'S ALL ABOUT INTERACTION
Whether text messaging your choice for the winner of *American Idol* or choosing a customized ending to a video game, technological interaction is an important tenet of modern culture. This was evident on a recent visit

to Disney's Magic Kingdom. For new attractions, the days of standing in line waiting are over. Parents receive pagers at the Dumbo ride, allowing children to explore a themed play area until their turn to climb into the flying elephant. At Belle's Magic Adventure, audience members become the cast, each person playing a role as the story unfolds. The underlying message is clear: our culture must connect to engage.

Technology's toolbox can provide the catalyst. Social media can help people interact during worship times and create networks within our ministries, lighting can help people connect emotionally with the theme of the worship time, and emerging video technology can engage worshippers and expand the touch of ministries as never before. To be successful in integration of these tools, however, we need a plan.

GOING FORWARD

Without a strategic plan, driven by the church's unified vision and purpose, the implementation of technology takes on a flavor-of-the-day approach. Daily marketers bombard us, pushing the next new thing or last-chance sales to buy the greatest piece of equipment ever invented. Without a clearly defined strategy, technology integration into our churches will be nothing more than random, and often incompatible, equipment purchases spread across various ministries of the church. During strategy development, we must ask these questions to determine what, if anything is needed:

- How does proposed new technology support the vision and purpose of our church?
- How will the new features or component, when implemented, enhance our worship times?
- Is it sustainable, in terms of acquisition and lifecycle cost, product lifecycle status, and leadership to operate it?
- How will our ministry and church family benefit?
- Will it strengthen relationships or build additional walls?
- Is it a good use of financial and people resources?
- Is this the right time to do this?

Today, innovations and advances in technology are often dated before they can be effectively implemented. What is new today is old tomorrow (and what is expensive today is cheaper tomorrow). As church leaders we must cautiously avoid jumping into every latest and greatest offering. While it may be amazing, it may not be needed now (or ever). Moving forward, we will see amazing developments in technology and media. Things that once were unimaginable will become common. These six suggestions will help worship leaders strategically plan for their churches:

1. **ORGANIZE A WORSHIP TECHNOLOGY TEAM.**—Worship leaders must surround themselves with individuals who understand the tools available and their potential to shape our worship experiences. These teams should be age-diverse and include people knowledgeable in various areas (web design, social media, mobile apps, television, audio, etc.). Most importantly, the team must focus on the vision and goals of the church at large rather than technology "just because." This requires a commitment by church leadership to provide opportunities for consistent discipleship, prayer, and vision casting.

2. **KNOW WHAT IS "OUT THERE."**—This is a huge challenge since available tools and their options change so rapidly. Your team must be immersed in the technology culture to stay current. Subscribe to technology magazines, read technology blogs, watch archived worship services, and visit other churches. Recently, 20 of our team leaders traveled to Dallas, Texas, to observe and learn from other churches (each person paid their own way). As part of that experience they witnessed an orchestra on a hydraulic lift, music-synced water shows, differing approaches to IMAG projection, environmental lighting, and an edited movie feature with an embedded sermon by the pastor. Was everything well received? No. Did it expand their understanding of the possibilities? Absolutely.

3. **TRAIN FOR SUCCESS.**—Our race to introduce new technological innovations is often at the expense of adequate training for those who will operate it. Technology introduced without proper training creates frustration for operators and users, and it may ultimately derail the entire process. We recently

rolled out a new worship ministry app for our church. As part of that process, our tech team insisted on an incremental rollout that allowed training time for those responsible for maintaining information, as well as the eventual users. Though it slowed the process, in the end it made for a smoother introduction and wider acceptance of the new tool. Make training a priority.

4. DON'T OVERDO IT.—Because so many options exist, we will overwhelm our people by offering too much at once. Prioritize new offerings, and systemically introduce them. While an overwhelming majority of people might be on Facebook, many have never heard of Instagram or Google+. And there will be a core group that will not touch a mobile device or personal computer. Select and prioritize focus areas then strategically move forward.

5. EVALUATE.—Simply because we successfully add a new technology tool to our worship services does not mean our work is over. Part of the process is to regularly reevaluate its effectiveness, both from operational and effectiveness points of view. Compare where you are to what new options are available. Keep a list of things to consider, and include those in this assessment. You may find something totally new is simply not as necessary as originally thought.

6. KEEP IT FRESH.—Social media and websites must not become stale, static pages of information. Stale information and repetitive information of limited use turns users away and actually detracts from other projects. Remember, perception is some folks' reality!

TECHNOLOGY MUST NOT OVERSHADOW RELATIONSHIPS

Our reliance on technology can work against the relationships we are trying to build within our ministries. While email and text messaging have characteristics of a personal contact, often their impact does not have the same influence as live communication. There are situations where in-person or voice-to-voice contact is critical. As our reliance on technologically driven communication rises, we are losing the ability to "read the room" and gauge responsiveness. We must have these important interpersonal relational skills to be effective in our ministries.

More critical, we must ensure our approaches to technology build relational walls within our ministries. A classic example is the robo-calls. When first introduced, many businesses (and churches) embraced this innovation as a great tool to inform people of meetings or for relating specific information about upcoming events. Prolonged exposure to the automated voice on the line, however, generated poor responses, making it apparent these were poor relational tools. What does it infer when our ministry members receive a computerized call? Are they not important enough to get a personal contact? Are we too busy to connect with them personally? If we say relationships are critical to the success of our ministries, but then have a computer make our phone calls, are we credible? This is an example of how a technology that, while useful, may not be beneficial for ministry.

DOES IT HELP CONNECT PEOPLE?

Modern technology, with its smartphones and social media, may provide some opportunities for people to connect more directly with worship experiences. Should we *encourage* the use of mobile devices? A growing number of people use these devices for every aspect of their lives. Why not encourage our members to download Bible apps and study tools? In some settings specific questions can be sent directly to the speaker for clarification or follow-up explanation. Sermon outlines can be posted that allow people to take notes and even interact with the message. QR codes can be used for people to scan (using a bar code reader app) for additional information on our ministries, eliminating the need for additional printed materials. Instagram accounts can be used to allow people attending church events to post photos and respond to their experiences. Tweets can provide daily updates, prayer requests, and rehearsal reminders. Private Facebook groups can be set up to allow prayer requests and concerns to be shared within the ministry family. The options are unlimited. Be creative and find ways for people to interact with your ministries.

CONCLUSION

Society is obsessed with technology. From smartphones to social media, all of us are influenced daily in almost every aspect of our lives. Throughout modern church history, technological advances were leveraged as tools to share the gospel. From the invention of radio and television, to the spread of the Internet, social media and Internet TV, technology has served as a functional tool in helping spread the gospel around the world.

Over the past two decades churches have struggled, and at times fought, over how much was too much. Church business meetings were punctuated with questions like, Do we really need a sound system? or Are projection screens really needed? Once embraced, however, few choose to revert back to earlier models.

The next decade will bring new opportunities and options, and these same questions will again dominate discussions. In the end, our decisions on what to integrate in worship must be driven by the role it serves in engaging people in a dialogue with God. We must remember that technology, like music, is simply a tool and not an end in itself. In far too many churches, however, technology has become the goal. We spend hours selecting it, determining its use, perfecting the presentation, and ensuring there are no glitches. Then we stand back with a sense of pride in our relevancy. Liberty University actually had a guest who encouraged our worship students to go for the cool factor. By the way, he has not been invited back.

Every week our churches are filled with deeply hurting people. The last thing they need is another light and video show to entertain them. The message of the Cross must be the driving force behind what we do. We need to ensure technology remains in its proper place. If we fail, the message of the gospel is undermined. That price is too great just to be cool!

CHAPTER 10

Every Nation, Every Tribe

THE EMERGENCE OF MULTICULTURAL WORSHIP

Give me your tired, your poor,
Your huddled masses yearning to breathe free,
The wretched refuse of your teeming shore,
Send these, the homeless, tempest-tossed to me,
I lift my lamp beside the golden door!
　　　　　　　—Emma Lazarus, "The New Colossus" (1883)

If you have visited Liberty Island in New York Harbor, the image of the Statue of Liberty, with her torch lifted as a beacon of freedom, is indelibly etched in your mind. The grand lady of liberty has welcomed newcomers to America's shores since 1886 and reminds all who pass within her shadow that we are a nation of immigrants. People come to the United States for many reasons. Early settlers left their native homelands in pursuit of religious freedom. Over the years others came in pursuit of fame, fortune, and the hope of new beginnings. Still others were brought to this nation in chains of slavery, thus becoming unwilling inhabitants of a new land. Regardless, they came by the millions, bringing unique perspectives and customs with them and eliminating the notion that cookie-cutter American citizens exist.

Ironically, this multiplicity of backgrounds, blended into a unique culture, defines the American experience. Once, it was said America had become a grand melting pot of cultures. While that may or may not have been true for some cultural groups who came to this country, many chose to maintain cultural nuances and differences with great pride. Others did so out of necessity for protection.

Eventually, though different parts of the nation were home to significant communities of those whose origins were African, eastern Asian, and Hispanic, a vast majority of United States citizens traced their roots primarily to European ancestry. We lived, worked, and went to school with others whose backgrounds were common to ours. Today, our neighborhoods, classrooms, and workplaces are a mix of different cultures, complete with custom and language differences. The transition has been progressive and visible. Just take a walk in your local park. The children playing together represent numerous cultural backgrounds. Even 20 years ago, that was far from the norm.

What is driving this demographic shift? The United States, over the past 40 years, witnessed the largest wave of immigration in our history. Pew Research (pewsocialtrends.org) states that 40 million new arrivals, mostly Hispanic and Asian immigrants, joined our nation, ushering in seismic shifts in our demographics. As a result, by 2020 there will be no single majority cultural group among children under the age of 18. According to Pew (pewsocialtrends.org), by 2050, "non-Hispanic whites," who currently comprise 63 percent of the total population, will decrease to less than half. Pew also reports that other "minority" groups will continue to grow as well:

> By 2050, the Hispanic share of the US population could be as high as 29%, up from 17% now. The black proportion of the population is projected to rise slightly to 13%, while the Asian share is projected to increase to 9% from its current 5%.

Interestingly, the US now has the second largest Hispanic population in the world.[1] The Hispanic population in the United States is more than 52 million and growing. The combined population in North America exceeds 56 million.[2]

These shifts will significantly influence worship over the next three decades. As communities become multilingual and more diverse overall, churches once filled with people who looked alike will be defined by their diversity. This will change the type of music used, the approach to language, and even the customs and traditions of local congregations.

BREAKDOWN OF THE HOMOGENEOUS UNIT PRINCIPLE

What does your church really look like? If answered honestly, congregations are often strikingly similar in general physical appearance, ethnic, and cultural composition. In fact, as Scott Thumma reported in *The Huffington Post* (huffingtonpost.com), the 2010 Faith Communities Today study (faithcommunitiestoday.com) coordinated by David Roozen at Hartford Institute for Religion Research (hartfordinstitute.org) indicates only 14 percent of congregations in the United States are "multiracial," defined as having at least 20 percent of members coming from groups recognized as different from the congregation's majority. If true, the follow-up question is obvious: why?

The Homogeneous Unit Principle (HUP), first espoused by renowned missiologist Donald A. McGavran, considered by many to be the founder of the modern-day church growth movement, is based on a belief that "people like to become Christians without crossing racial, linguistic, or class barriers."[3] While the term describes actual church practice, HUP was an intentional strategy used by many churches. Terms such as *target group* evolved from this approach and defined church growth strategies such as Willow Creek's unchurched "Harry and Mary." Sadly, HUP was used to justify racial or ethnic discrimination by churches unwilling to reach out to certain groups. With the shifts in demographics, however, nondiverse churches no longer reflect the makeup of our communities and appear exclusive and disconnected to younger generations.

As Sam Rainer points out in "10 (Unexpected) Church Trends to Surface by 2020" (churchleaders.com), diversity is a way of life for millennials. Accordingly, millennials expect churches to represent this diversity. Plus, it's biblical. Over the next decade for a church to be successful, it must redefine itself within this context. Rainer contends that the explosion of the heterogeneous church may be the most significant emerging trend for churches over the next decade:

> As the younger generation ages, they will not be represented by the homogeneous unit principle that was championed in the early years of the church growth movement. Basically, this principle states that people desire to worship and serve in church with similar people, and the best way to reach people is with others who are "similar."
>
> Boomers began to change this thinking. Many sought diversity—they intentionally championed it. For many Millennials, diversity (or heterogeneity) is normal. In the future, homogenous units will still form. . . . People with common interests, characteristics, life stages, and languages will still gravitate towards each other. The difference with the younger generation is that these divides will not be as distinct, specifically in ethnic terms, . . . The Millennial generation will gravitate towards heterogeneous churches because they represent what is normal in their generation.

This cannot be emphasized enough. Many within our churches, with a good heart and spirit, think that Christianity needs to be "colorblind." In the twenty-first century, many cultural groups see that as condescending and insensitive. Some sociologists are talking about retroactive acculturalization whereby many groups are now proudly emphasizing their cultural differences and encouraging their people groups to proudly and sometimes strongly return to their cultural roots. Churches must be respectful of cultural differences and help every culture celebrate that which makes them unique. Does that come at a price? Yes. Does it make it difficult for some people? Yes. We are not talking about theological challenges, which we will talk about in just a moment. We are simply talking about cultural sensitivity and kindness toward others who are different.

THEOLOGICAL CONFUSION

While cultural diversity brings many advantages, it presents theological challenges. When Lavon and his family relocated to Lynchburg to teach at Liberty University, they lived in an apartment complex near the university. The international flavor was striking, with residents representing many cultures, languages, and nations. One evening the Grays discovered their youngest daughter, Katibeth (who was six years old at the time), seated with her legs crossed in a classic Hindu meditation position, making a low humming noise. She obviously had been influenced by her young Indian friend who lived a few apartments down. While this situation provided a teachable moment on Hinduism, it also underscored the potential influence of a multicultural community on everyday life.

As we reach out to the international community now residing at the doorsteps of our churches, Christians will be confronted with belief systems foreign to them: Islam, Buddhism, Hinduism, Mormonism, and New Age, just to name a few. Most Christians have little understanding of these religions' teachings and are ill equipped to answer questions of theology and doctrine when placed in mentoring or discipling relationships. Absent proper theological grounding, this is a fertile ground for errant doctrine. This issue reinforces the importance of sound theological content within the songs we choose for worship. Church leaders must intentionally disciple their members in the foundations of Christianity in order to properly equip them for the theological diversity of the next decade.

INCREASED SENSITIVITY

Our culture's diversity, as well as a heightened sense of political correctness, has prompted intense discussions regarding racial and ethnic sensitivity. Athletic teams, such as the Washington Redskins, Atlanta Braves, and Cleveland Indians have come under fire for mascots and team names offensive to American Indians. Other schools, such as the University of Mississippi, changed their mascots because of perceived connections to past racial failings.

This subject impacted denominational entities including Southern Baptists. In November 2013, Thom Rainer, president of LifeWay Christian Resources, issued an apology to Asian Americans for the publishing of *Rickshaw Rally* some ten years earlier. The children's musical, designed for use in Vacation Bible School, used racial stereotypes that offended many in the Asian American community. Sarah Pulliam Bailey of Religious News Service reported that Rainer made his comments as part of Mosaix, a multiethnic church conference in Long Beach, California, that attracted more than 1,000 people from around the United States.

> I am sincerely sorry stereotypes were used in our materials, and I apologize for the pain they caused. . . . I agree with those who have helped us understand the offensive nature of that material. And I agree evangelical church and ministry leaders—particularly those of us who are white—need to commit to assuring, as best we can, these offenses stop.

Some may argue these are examples of out-of-control pursuit of political correctness. In reality, our culture is more sensitive to these issues than ever before in history. Trite or patronizing approaches to multicultural worship will be emphatically rejected. Our efforts to integrate cultures within a unified worship experience must be prayerfully and thoughtfully approached with a focus on doctrine, musical excellence, and plausible presentation. Anything less is unacceptable.

♪ A BIBLICAL RESPONSE

Diversity is an important part of biblical history. Beginning with creation, uniqueness, and distinctiveness were a part of God's plan for mankind. Paul refers to this in Acts 17:26, when he stated, "From one man He has made every nationality to live over the whole earth and has determined their appointed times and the boundaries of where they live." Different ethnicities were part of God's plan from the time Adam and Eve occupied the Garden of Eden. Solomon, as recorded in 1 Kings 8:41–43, during the dedication of the Temple prayed that Gentiles would hear of God's great name:

> Even for the foreigner who is not of Your people Israel but has come from a distant land because of Your name—for they will hear of Your great name, mighty hand, and outstretched arm, and will come and pray toward this temple—may You hear in heaven, Your dwelling place, and do according to all the foreigner asks You for. Then all the people on earth will know Your name, to fear You as Your people Israel do and know that this temple I have built is called by Your name.

Psalm 86:9 further underscores the demand of unified worship by different ethnicities: "All the nations You have made will come and bow down before You, Lord, and will honor Your name."

In the New Testament, Jesus served as the unblemished example of multicultural ministry. Eight days following His birth, Simeon acknowledged the fulfillment of prophecy by referring to the Christ child as "a light for revelation to the Gentiles and glory to Your people Israel" (Luke 2: 32). The ministry of Jesus was marked by the crossing of racial and ethnic boundaries. Whether it was the Samaritan woman or a Roman centurion, Jesus offered salvation to Jew and Gentile alike. Following His crucifixion and resurrection, He instructed the disciples to follow His example to "make disciples of all nations" (Matthew 28:19).

Following Jesus' instruction, the disciples led in spreading the gospel across the continent. The day of Pentecost, described in Acts 2, serves as a pivotal point for multicultural worship and reminds us of worship's potential to unify people across multicultural lines:

> There were Jews living in Jerusalem, devout men from every nation under heaven. When this sound occurred [rushing wind], a crowd came together and was confused because each one heard them speaking in his own language. And they were astounded and amazed, saying, "Look, aren't all these who are speaking Galileans? How is it that each of us can hear in our own native language? Parthians, Medes, Elamites; those who live in Mesopotamia, in Judea and Cappadocia, Pontus and Asia, Phrygia and Pamphylia, Egypt and the parts of Libya near Cyrene; visitors from Rome, both Jews and proselytes, Cretans and Arabs—we hear them speaking the magnificent acts of God in our own languages." They were all astounded and perplexed, saying to one another, "What could this be?"
>
> (vv. 5–12)

Centuries earlier God confused the languages as punishment at the Tower of Babel. In Acts 2, He used different languages to unite the people with the message of Christ. This event was central in the spreading of the gospel across the known world as those present carried the message to different parts of the world.

Once we understand that God created the nations and desires unified worship, our perspective on multicultural worship begins to shift. One need only look to the Book of Revelation to get a glimpse of heavenly worship, in which cultural and ethnic boundaries will be no more:

> After this I looked, and there was a vast multitude from every nation, tribe, people, and language, which no one could

*number, standing before the throne and before the Lamb.
They were robed in white with palm branches in their hands.
And they cried out in a loud voice: Salvation belongs to our
God, who is seated on the throne, and to the Lamb!*

(Revelation 7:9–10)

𝄢 WHAT NOW?

There should be no confusion concerning God's mandate to reach our communities with the message of Christ: the requirement is clear. When churches acknowledge the changing identities of their communities, reaching across cultural barriers becomes a question of obedience. At its core the issue is spiritual. Will we reach those around us, as directed by Scripture, or we will choose to ignore their existence simply because it moves us from our comfort zones? Once we acknowledge and obey, the focus shifts to how. The methodologies are pragmatic in nature and can be adjusted to reflect the real demographics of our communities and involve financial and administrative decisions in determining how to proceed.

Just as we have no silver bullet for unifying congregations in multigenerational worship, specific approaches to a multicultural worship are varied and reflective of individual communities. There is no one-size-fits-all approach. Though a method works in one setting, there is no guarantee of its success in another. Church leaders must prayerfully seek God's direction for their unique situation, resulting in a wide variety of approaches. The following principles will assist church leaders in guiding their churches through the multicultural influences that will shape worship over the next decade.

KNOW YOUR COMMUNITY

Albert Einstein is credited with defining *insanity* as "doing the same thing over and over again and expecting different results." Unfortunately, many churches use this approach to understand and reach their communities. Churches often continue to conduct business as usual, with little regard for changing demographics.

First Baptist Church, Jackson, Mississippi, is located downtown and sits across the street from the state capitol. Organized in 1838, First Baptist Jackson has a rich heritage and stood as a model of missions and ministry for more than 175 years. With this understanding, however, developing vision, goals, and strategy while ignoring that Jackson has a steadily declining European American population (28.2 percent as of the 2012 census), down 20 percent since 1990, would be ludicrous.[4] With a church membership that is 98 percent "white," First Baptist Jackson's direction over the ensuing years must reflect an intentional strategy to reach the community where it sits today. The strategy can only develop by answering critical questions such as:

- What is the population of the surrounding community?
- What is the cultural/ethnic makeup of our community?
- What does our community look like? (age, gender, marital status)
- What are the educational and economic levels of our community?
- What are the religious affiliations of our community
- What is the average income of those in our community?
- What is the age and household makeup of those in our community?
- And most importantly: does our church membership accurately reflect our community?

Church leaders must accurately define their surrounding culture and then prayerfully develop evangelistic strategies for reaching that culture for Christ. Once defined, worship pastors must design worship experiences that connect with the changing demographic. The potential for conflict is huge and includes, among other issues, language, and musical style preferences.

DIVERSIFY THE LEADERSHIP

When attempting to engage worshippers through a multicultural approach, the leadership team must accurately reflect the demographic makeup of those within the church and surrounding community. Worship leaders, musicians, singers, and staff must represent different ethnicities and cultural backgrounds to have credibility. Several years ago we attempted to launch a satellite campus in Jackson targeted specifically at reaching the African American community. We secured a building, purchased equipment, and planned outreach strategies. There was one major problem: our understanding of the African American culture was dismal! To be blunt, we had a group of middle-aged European American men attempting to develop an evangelism strategy to reach underprivileged African American teens. In a city with a long history of racial discrimination, it is not surprising we were looked at with suspicion. We did not understand the culture and provided no means of breaking down barriers. While our intentions were honorable, this effort was a total failure.

Where did we go wrong? We failed to bring the right people to the table. While we did call an African American pastor with much experience in working with Southern Baptist churches within the African American community, his role in strategy and identity development was limited. Even our worship team and band consisted of hired singers to transfer the same quality level as our downtown campus to the new location. In the end, our satellite effort more closely resembled a "little First Baptist Jackson" than an inner-city missions effort. We honestly wanted to reach the African American community, but insisted it be on our terms. From the outset, the effort was doomed.

Churches serious about reaching their communities commit to reshape their leadership teams to accurately reflect the people groups around them. This includes diverse senior leadership teams that directly influence the church's vision and strategy. This approach breaks downs barriers and creates buy-in to our ministry goals. Otherwise, we will not be successful.

PLANT NEW CHURCHES

The North American Mission Board has an ambitious goal of planting 15,000 new churches in North America in the next ten years. Local churches are best equipped to plant local churches. In *Aliens in the Promised Land: Why Minority Leadership Is Overlooked in White Christian Churches and Institutions* (edited by Anthony B. Bradley, P & R Publishing Co.: Phillipsburg, NJ, 2013), essayist Lance Lewis points out that many church planting efforts fail because of the lack of understanding of the culture. He also rightly points out that we often ignore existing churches in particular areas because we are unaware of those groups and fail in church planting because we have not taken into consideration the wonderful work already occurring in a certain area, even if it is outside our denominational structure.

Recognizing cultural differences and issues are paramount in starting new churches. While at Taylors First Baptist Church, we intentionally planted new churches trying to be sensitive to those in particular areas. Sometimes it might be a blue-collar area in which one should never put in a white-collar pastor or a heavily Hispanic area that obviously calls for sensitivity. Often we think because someone speaks Spanish, they can relate to anyone of a Hispanic or a Latino background. That is patently untrue. Cultural differences occur even within every subgroup, and sensitivity must be practiced even in those arenas.

TEAR DOWN THE WALLS

While most are hesitant to admit it, years of racial and ethnic prejudice have built major obstacles to many in our communities. To break down these obstacles requires consistent effort, communication, and coordinated action. Even though First Baptist Jackson's satellite campus failed, leaders in the community noticed our effort. As a result, the leadership of the Grammy Award–winning Mississippi Mass Choir approached us about the possibility of a live recording featuring their choir with the choir and orchestra of First Baptist Jackson. After months of planning and rehearsals, one of the most memorable sights in the history of our church was to see our combined choirs, with over four hundred voices, singing "God Gets the Glory" to a standing-room-only crowd in the sanctuary of First Baptist Jackson. As we looked around the sanctuary that night, the reality that many of the singers, as well as those in the congregation, would not have been allowed in the building prior to 1970, did not escape those of us in leadership. Walls were being torn down.

Following the event, area pastors shared that this event did more for race relations in the city of Jackson than anything in recent memory. Was all racial tension forever healed? No. Did we make strides to reconciliation? Absolutely! Tearing down walls constructed over many years takes time, energy, and cooperation, but it can happen. Churches simply must be willing to take the first steps.

BE INTENTIONAL

Engaging in multicultural worship will not happen without intentionality. This requires a clear vision consistently articulated to the church, as well as a worship planning strategy that systematically models excellence and diversity. Without these elements, leaders and church members revert to their comfort zones and lose focus.

One of the early steps in making this shift is encouraging existing ministries to diversify their teams from within. This requires enormous energy devoted to recruitment, retention, and mentoring, but the relationships developed are worth the effort. Most communities are filled with musicians representing a wide range of cultural diversity. In addition, many churches have members with musical skills, who are part of groups that are in the minority in their church. Find these musicians, and plug them into your ministries.

BRIDGE THE LANGUAGE GAP

Language is the vehicle for communication and central to worship. We must cautiously not force people into a worship approach that robs them of their ability to respond to God's revelation. If people do not understand the language, it limits their ability to engage in the worship experience.

As a growing number of languages and cultures are represented in our churches, worship leaders must develop methodologies for breaking down the language barriers. While some churches use live translators on the platform, technology supports other options for sermons and music to be translated and broadcast to worshippers via electronic hearing devices. Other churches project multiple translations of worship songs on screens allowing different ethnicities to worship in their heart language. Other options, including art, digital imagery, and sign language, are being utilized to tear down these barriers. As technology advances, more options will emerge. Church leaders with diverse congregations must creatively explore all delivery options to engage as many people as possible in the worship experience.

The language factor was reinforced several years ago on a music missions trip to Ukraine. One evening the choir presented a concert in a rented theater on the outskirts of the city. Seated near the front was an elderly woman, her face marked by years of poverty and oppression, who mouthed the words to some of the songs in her native language as tears ran down her cheeks. Because our choir made the effort to learn the songs in Russian, she was able to join in worship using her native language.

When our ability to understand the language is removed, it becomes difficult to participate in the worship dialogue. Most often we become observers of other people worshipping. As church leaders we must ensure our methods do not force people into nonparticipatory roles in order to meet our personal ministry objectives.

IT IS NOT ALL OR NOTHING

Some argue the only option for multicultural worship is a joint experience comprised of all cultures and ethnicities. Other congregations encourage non-English-speaking worship times in addition to their unified service, which brings everyone together in the same room. Another model allows different weekly services, with monthly multicultural worship times using a wide range of music and cultural elements. All have experienced some level of success.

In reality, our approaches will be debated and changed over time based on successes and failures, and through the use of advancing technological options. The key issue is that church leaders make a decision to reach demographically diverse communities, and then develop intentional strategies to engage in multicultural worship experiences consistently. Regardless, our "tools" must never displace the voice of the worshipper.

CONCLUSION

The enormous demographic shifts of the past four decades changed the face of communities across the United States. Many churches are left with congregations that stand in stark contrast to the demographic realities of their surrounding communities. While homogeneous church models create a sense of comfort, they do not resonate with younger generations whose lives are characterized by diversity. More importantly, they fail to reach entire segments of our population who reside at the doorsteps of our churches, an affront to the mandate of the Great Commission.

Old methodologies, often defined by separate congregations based on ethnicity, and racial thinking, are foreign to those who grew up as part of the cultural mosaic of the past 20 years. Churches refusing to develop intentional strategies to integrate cultures will find themselves largely irrelevant to the 80 million millennials who represent the largest non-Christian group in the history of the United States. Left unchecked, the continuing decline of American Christianity leaves our churches as empty relics to failed methodologies.

There is a better plan. Worship pastors must develop intentional strategies to diversify their leadership teams, expand their worship palette, and tear down the walls that have divided us far too long. We must focus on building unity, rather than supporting barriers that inhibit the spread of the gospel. Jesus died for all people, to redeem a human race of every tribe, language, and culture. His sacrifice demands we unify the body of Christ in worship to Him. When this happens, we can join with the heavenly hosts in singing a new song of praise to the King of kings and Lord of lords:

> *You are worthy to take the scroll and to open its seals, because You were slaughtered, and You redeemed people for God by Your blood from every tribe and language and people and nation.*
>
> (Revelation 5:9)

Notes

CHAPTER 2

[1] C. S. Lewis, as cited by Art Lindsley in "C. S. Lewis on Chronological Snobbery," *Knowing and Doing* (Springfield, VA: C. S. Lewis Institute), Spring 2003, 1, http://www.cslewisinstitute.org/webfm_send/47, accessed July 2, 2013.

[2] "NAMB, States Target Church Stagnation, Decline," Baptist Press, accessed March 17, 2014, http://www.bpnews.net/BPnews.asp?ID=38800.

[3] Charles Quarles, "Southern Baptists Must Learn to 'Choose Our Battles Wisely,'" *The Baptist Message Online*, accessed March, 28, 2013, http://www.baptistmessage.com/node/7527.

[4] Ibid.

CHAPTER 4

[1] Larry Eskridge, "The 'Praise and Worship' Revolution, *Christianity Today*, Christian History, http://www.christianitytoday.com/ch/thepastinthepresent/storybehind/praiseworshiprevolution.html, accessed October 2, 2013.

[2] Elmer L. Towns and Vernon M. Whaley, *Worship Through the Ages: How the Great Awakenings Shape Evangelical Worship* (Nashville: B & H Academic, 2012), 329.

[3] Vernon Whaley, "Equipping Students with Modern Skills: Balancing Traditional Standards and Cultural Demands" (paper delivered at the Building the Next Generation of Worship Leaders Conference at Baylor University, Waco, TX, September 27–29, 2012).

[4] Ibid.

[5] Ibid.

[6]Ibid.

[7]Ibid.

[8]Ibid.

[9]Ibid.

[10]Ibid.

[11]Ibid.

CHAPTER 7

[1]Josh Burek, "Christian Faith: Calvinism Is Back," *The Christian Science Monitor*, March 27, 2010, 7, http://search.proquest.com/docview/405576011?accoun tid=12085.

[2]Adapted from the doctrinal statement of Liberty University. The statement can be found in its entirety at https://www.liberty.edu/aboutliberty/?PID=6907.

CHAPTER 9

[1]Kathryn Zickuhr and Mary Madden, "Older Adults and Internet Use," Pew Research Internet Project, accessed November 20, 2013, http://www .pewinternet.org/Reports/2012/Older-adults-and-internet-use.aspx.

[2]See http://www.webmd.com/mental-health/features/when-technology -addiction-takes-over-your-life?print=true, accessed November 21, 2013.

CHAPTER 10

[1]It has surpassed Spain and now only Mexico has a larger Hispanic population than the United States.

[2]Pew Research Center, Hispanic Center Tabulations for the 2000 Census and the 2010 American Community Survey.

[3]See http://www.baylor.edu/content/services/document.php/110989.pdf, accessed March 15, 2014.

[4]See http://quickfacts.census.gov/qfd/states/28/28049.html, accessed October 15, 2013.

*New Hope® Publishers is a division of WMU®, an international orga-
nization that challenges Christian believers to understand and be radically
involved in God's mission. For more information about WMU,
go to wmu.com. More information about New Hope books may be
found at NewHopeDigital.com. New Hope books may be
purchased at your local bookstore.*

Use the QR reader on your
smartphone to visit us online at
NewHopeDigital.com

If you've been blessed by this book, we would like to hear your story.
The publisher and author welcome your comments and
suggestions at: newhopereader@wmu.org.

Leadership Resources to Challenge and Equip

The Nehemiah Factor
16 Vital Keys to Living Like a Missional Leader
DR. FRANK S. PAGE
978-1-59669-375-3
$16.99

Upside-Down Leadership
Rethinking Influence and Success
TAYLOR FIELD
978-1-59669-342-5
$14.99

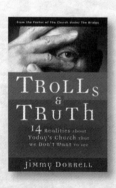

Trolls & Truth
14 Realities About Today's Church
That We Don't Want to See
JIMMY DORRELL
978-1-59669-010-3
$14.99

For more information on these books and our authors visit
NewHopeDigital.com.

Download our FREE New Hope app to receive daily devotions, chapter
samples, articles, and more!